Creating the Full-Service Homework Center in Your Library

Cindy Mediavilla

AMERICAN LIBRARY ASSOCIATION
Chicago and London
2001

While extensive effort has gone into ensuring the reliability of information appearing in this book, the publisher makes no warranty, express or implied, on the accuracy or reliability of the information, and does not assume and hereby disclaims any liability to any person for any loss or damage caused by errors or omissions in this publication.

Project editor: Eloise L. Kinney

Text and cover design: Dianne M. Rooney

Composition: ALA Editions using Goudy and Korinna typefaces

Printed on 50-pound white offset, a pH-neutral stock, and bound in 10-point cover stock by McNaughton & Gunn.

The paper used in this publication meets the minimum requirements of American National Standard for Information Sciences—Permanence of Paper for Printed Library Materials, ANSI Z39.48-1992. ⊚

Library of Congress Cataloging-in-Publication Data

Mediavilla, Cindy, 1953–
    Creating the full-service homework center in your library / Cindy Mediavilla.
      p.   cm.
    Includes bibliographical references and index.
    ISBN 0-8389-0800-4 (alk. paper)
      1. Homework centers in libraries—United States. 2. Public libraries—Services to students—United States. 3. Homework—United States—Library resources. 4. Latchkey children—Services for—United States. I. Title.

Z718.7.M44 2001
027.4'0973—dc21   00-052163

Printed in the United States of America

05 04 03 02 01   5 4 3 2 1

CONTENTS

Contents

ACKNOWLEDGMENTS

I have many people to thank for supporting and enflaming my interest in homework centers. First and foremost, I want to thank former Orange Public Library director Karen Leo for having the vision to create the Friendly Stop and Anthony Garcia, former Friendly Stop manager, for inspiring in me a love of working with young people. I am also most grateful to Professor Virginia Walter for encouraging me to continue my research on homework centers despite a major change in my doctoral emphasis.

I must also thank Mary Jo Lynch and the other members of the Fyan Committee, who realized the value in my studying after-school homework-assistance programs and so granted me a Loleta D. Fyan Research Grant in 1998 to complete my research. I am also indebted to the staff of all the libraries I visited—both virtually and in person—without whom this book would not be possible: Penny Markey, Josephine Zoretich, and Patrick Palma of the County of Los Angeles Public Library; Jeanine Asche, Jesus Valle, Barbara Escoffier, and Susan Goetz of San Mateo County Library System, California; Sally Childs and Shirley Dawson of Monterey County Free Libraries, California; Kim Bui-Burton, Karen Brown, and Dina Stansbury of Monterey Public Library, California; Patricia Lichter and Patricia M. Wong of Oakland Public Library; Barbara Alesandrini, formerly of Oakland Public Library; Kit Willis and Lisa Meeker of the County of Ventura Library Services Agency, California; Lori Hopkins of Rancho Cucamonga Public Library, California; Sheri Irvin and Carolyn Denny of Riverside Public Library, California; Terry Chekon, Phyllis Martin, and Maria Griego of Sacramento Public Library; Susan Erickson of San Bernardino County Library, California; Audrey Jones of San Diego County Library; Ana Lindner of South San Francisco Public Library; Natalie Renscher, formerly of San Jose Public Library, California; Dana Burton and Anna Gercas of Monroe County Public Library, Indiana; Kat Kan and Suzanne Murray of Allen County Public Library, Indiana; Deborah Taylor and Eunice Harper of the Enoch Pratt Free Library, Maryland; Sandy Souza of the Massachusetts Board of Library Commissioners; Penny Johnson of Hennepin County

Library, Minnesota; Sara Waters and Cathy Hoffman of Minneapolis Public Library; Leesa Wisdorf of Northfield Public Library, Minnesota; Doug Wooley and Barbara Auerbach of Brooklyn Public Library; Kathleen Cronin of New Rochelle Public Library, New York; Margaret Tice and Roseanne Cerny of Queens Borough Public Library; Sami Scripter of Multnomah County Library, Oregon; Marin Younker of Tigard Public Library, Oregon; Patrick Jones of Houston Public Library; and Bonnie Worcester of Fairfax County Public Library, Virginia.

Finally, with deepest gratitude, I thank my husband, Tim Ahern, for continually supporting my efforts even when my research took me far from home for many days at a time.

INTRODUCTION

I became interested in homework-assistance programs in the early 1990s when I was hired by the Orange Public Library, in California, to administer both the central library and a federally funded program called *La Pareda de Amistad*, the Friendly Stop, a homework center located in the heart of a Latino barrio. That experience had a profound effect on my professional outlook. Not only was this the first time I had ever directly worked with young adults, but the rewards were immediate as I watched students' reading skills develop and grades improve. In fact, so gratifying was my experience that, when I left the city of Orange in 1993, I initiated plans to become a doctoral student in hopes of creating an instrument to measure the effectiveness of homework-assistance programs in public libraries. Although I eventually changed the emphasis of my doctoral research, I never abandoned my fascination with homework centers; and so, in 1998, I applied for and received the American Library Association's Loleta D. Fyan Award to survey homework-assistance programs in public libraries across the country. This book is the result of that study.

A Historical Overview

Although formalized homework "centers" are a relatively recent phenomenon in public libraries, the idea of librarians meeting the curriculum-based needs of young students is, of course, not at all new. As early as 1898, forward-looking public librarians emphasized the importance of helping children with their schoolwork. In a speech before the Ohio Library Association, librarian Linda Anne Eastman admonished that one of the requisites for working successfully with children was a thorough knowledge of the school's curriculum. Thus, many turn-of-the-century children's departments not only introduced good books to youngsters, but also reinforced and enriched school class work.

For many years, public librarians gladly assumed the role of homework facilitators. As library director Lesley Newton noted in 1932, reference work and collection development were often dictated by the course of study offered in the community's schools. According to pioneer children's librarian Effie Power, library staff in the early '40s spent an inordinate amount of time helping kids with their class assignments. To meet this growing demand, public librarians regularly reserved special copies of supplementary school reading, borrowed books from the state library for student use, acquired school reading lists and advance copies of assignments, communicated regularly with nearby schools through visits and newsletters, and, in some cases, even maintained a separate reference room for high-school students.

No wonder, then, that the public library became something of a haven for students of all ages in the post–World War II era. During this period, children knew that when the school day was over, the public library was always there to welcome them. Indeed, the library was often the only place in town for the child to go other than the movies or the street. Yet by the late '50s, many public librarians had become disenchanted with serving young people. Thanks to the postwar "baby boom," more children than ever were enrolled in school. This, combined with a nationwide fervor to win the international "space race," prompted educators to revamp their curricula, sending thousands of youngsters into their local public libraries for after-school homework assistance. At the Enoch Pratt Free Library in Baltimore, more than half the library's patrons were students using the collection to complete school-related assignments. Meanwhile, in California, youth were flocking to local libraries in greater numbers than ever before. The overcrowding became so extreme that Los Angeles Public Library director Harold Hamill proclaimed that heavy student use was turning his facilities into an extension of school libraries. The public library was not equipped to handle increasing student usage.

To control what became known as "the student problem," public librarians began limiting use of their libraries in the early '60s. According to findings revealed at the 1967 American Library Association (ALA) Conference, young people's borrowing privileges were being restricted nationwide. Reference service to students was curtailed or denied altogether; library use permits were required from teachers or parents or both; teenagers were limited to certain hours and areas of the library; and boys and girls in many towns were not allowed to use their local libraries on the same evenings. In her landmark book *A Fair Garden and the Swarm of Beasts*, young adult librarian Margaret A. Edwards lamented the public library's neglect of the city teenager. Citing a 1967 study by the ALA Ad Hoc Committee on Instruction in the Use of Libraries, she noted that one of the greatest barriers to full public library service was the poor attitude of public librarians toward students. Youngsters, in fact, complained that they were often mistreated by library staff. As one maligned student commented, librarians who offered help in a pleasant manner were much less common than those who made kids feel ignorant.

The antagonism of the late '60s between public librarians and their young patrons left a lingering residuum that, in some organizations, still manifests itself in restricted student privileges. In fact, many public librarians feel that curriculum-based library services are best left to the schools. Other librarians, however, have begun to understand just how interrelated academic and public library services are. In California, for example, successful homework-help programs have flourished since the mid-'80s. One of the earliest was Project My Turn, an after-school program that paired junior-high kids with high-school-aged tutors. Run by the National City Public Library, the program helped older as well as younger teens develop stronger literacy and homework-related skills. In Long Beach, the public library's After-School Study Center, funded through a California State Library Partnerships for Change grant, effectively targeted Cambodian immigrant children, who otherwise would not have received homework assistance because of language barriers and a lack of resources at home.

An after-school homework-assistance program developed in the early '90s by the Monterey County Free Libraries still thrives in California. Responding to an overwhelming number of unsupervised "latchkey children" arriving daily after school, branch librarian Rosellen Brewer petitioned a local foundation to sponsor a homework center in her library. Today twelve of Monterey County's seventeen branches offer after-school homework assistance. Severe latchkey problems have also prompted librarians to establish homework-focused programs in Queens Borough, New York; Atlanta and Dekalb County, Georgia; Durham County, North Carolina; Weber County, Utah; and Seattle. Often staffed by volunteers or community-paid workers, these programs offer one-on-one homework assistance while lifting some of the librarian's daily burden.

Although after-school programs for younger kids tend to be motivated by a need to control overflowing numbers of library users, homework assistance for teens is usually instigated in hopes of attracting older kids who are reluctant to use the library. Two of the most noteworthy teen programs, which offer math tutoring at the Monroe County, Indiana, and Brooklyn public libraries, have received the Young Adult Library Services Association (YALSA) Excellence in Library Services to Young Adults Project award. Other recent winners of the YALSA award include Houston Public Library's ASPIRE (After School Programs Inspire Reading Enrichment), Oakland Public Library's PASS! (Partners for Achieving School Success), and Castroville Library's Homework Center in California.

About This Book

Despite a growing interest in the topic, little has been written about after-school homework-assistance programs in the professional literature. The few pieces that do exist are descriptive rather than evaluative, limiting their usefulness as planning tools. Therefore, when librarians are faced with launching a new homework center, they generally post a query on their favorite discussion group and hope that someone will respond with knowledgeable advice.

To visit as large and varied a sample of libraries as possible, I posted my own query on the Public Libraries, Young Adults, and Children (PUBYAC) discussion group, requesting the names of exemplary after-school homework programs. I also posted a similar message on CALIX, the California Library Association's discussion group, and directly contacted those few programs that had been written about in the library literature. In all, I visited twenty-three library jurisdictions—twelve in California, five on the East Coast, five in the Midwest, and one in Oregon—and established countless "virtual" relationships with like-minded librarians via e-mail. What I found, during the course of my research, was that although various homework centers share certain elements, no two programs are exactly alike. Indeed, the most successful programs are those that reflect their particular communities and so, out of necessity, are unique. The notion of a homework center differs, therefore, from library to library.

For the purpose of this book I have defined *homework center* as a program dedicated to meeting the curricular needs of students by providing

- staff or volunteers who are trained to assist students with their homework,
- space designated for student use during specific days and times, and
- a multiformat collection of materials related to the curricular needs of students.

Reflecting this definition, this book is organized by the various components required to administer an effective homework center. In separate chapters I discuss needs assessment; service plan; staff and volunteer recruitment; job duties and training; funding and partnerships; collaboration with schools; space and location; service hours; programming and corollary services; collection development; supplies and equipment; security and liability issues; media and public relations; and methods of assessing effectiveness. Gathered in appendixes at the back of the book are sample assessment tools, homework-center goals and objectives, volunteer-recruitment materials and applications, homework-helper contracts, job descriptions, grant applications, registration forms, and more.

In addition, I have included profiles of ten homework-assistance programs that exemplify various organizational and funding scenarios. Although all the homework centers I visited are worthy of commendation, these ten libraries have been singled out because they represent a variety of model programs, ranging from shoestring operations run on very little money to fully funded projects. Hopefully readers will be able to "mix and match" relevant aspects from each library scenario and combine them to create even more unique homework-center models, based on their own communities' needs.

1

Why Homework Centers?

Although no two homework centers are completely alike, the motivation for developing such programs is strikingly similar throughout the country. Reasons for establishing formal homework help are either internally driven, such as the library's need to control overwhelming numbers of unattended children, or motivated by external forces, such as a citywide mandate to offer after-school prevention programs. In all cases, the homework center is viewed as a solution to one or more problems involving youth. At the very least, the homework center offers kids a designated place to go after school where they can get help with their school assignments. At its best, the homework-assistance program offers positive human interaction and scholastic support that might otherwise be missing from the youngster's life.

The need for community-based after-school programs is well established. In 1992, the Carnegie Council on Adolescent Development published a report revealing that the most dangerous time of day for youth are the three hours following school. During this period, kids are more susceptible to giving in to negative peer pressure and engaging in illegal activities. For this reason, the Carnegie group recommended that communities create support networks for young adolescents, including after-school programs where kids can acquire useful experiences to promote healthy growth and development. Any number of adult community leaders, including librarians, should serve as agents in this process.

In a 2000 study, the national offices of the U.S. Department of Education and U.S. Department of Justice found that children who are left alone after school have more difficulties with their class work than those who participate in after-school programs. Not only are the latter group of students more likely to succeed academically, but they are also much more self-confident. In addition, these children are more likely to develop stronger social skills and learn how to acceptably handle conflicts. To be effective, after-school programs must help develop relationships between youth and caring adults, as well as build partnerships with families, schools, and communities. Strong programs also provide enriching learning activities while offering a safe and healthy after-school environment.

Homework and the Public Library

Homework serves many purposes in a student's life. It reinforces classroom learning while allowing the youngster time for creativity and deeper exploration. School assignments also help build organizational and time-management skills, as well as subject expertise. Perhaps even more importantly, homework provides the opportunity for one to learn how to work independently.

Successfully completing school assignments can be extremely stressful, however, especially if the student lacks the resources to succeed. Academic excellence may allow one to attend the college of one's choice and may even lead to a high-paying job after graduation, but kids need help obtaining their scholastic goals. Unfortunately, today's parents do not always know what their children are studying, nor do they have the time, energy, or the skills to help their kids learn to read or do math. Low-income families may also lack the sophisticated resources required these days to compete academically in school. Combine this with a home environment where English is a second language, and the child has no alternative but to seek homework assistance elsewhere. No wonder then that public libraries target the homework needs of students, especially those from low-income and immigrant communities.

Although only one in seven public libraries currently offers formal after-school homework assistance, the American Library Association (ALA) anticipates, in a study conducted in 1999, that the need for homework-related library services will increase in the coming years. Indeed, the expansion of such programs seems only natural. The American people overwhelmingly believe in the educational role of the library, and, in fact, 60 percent of public library users are under the age of eighteen. In the Public Library Association's 1998 planning document, compiled by Ethel Himmel and William James Wilson, homework-assistance programs are included as a major component of the updated educational support role. Those libraries officially adopting this service agree to provide resources and personal assistance to facilitate students' educational progress. In addition, "formal learning support" libraries may provide Internet access, expert homework assistance and tutoring, group study rooms, and computer labs.

Besides staff, space, and a collection, homework-friendly public libraries also offer an educationally conducive, more flexible environment in which to study. Although on-campus after-school programs are often negatively associated with remedial learning or detention, public library homework centers are considered a "cool" place to go, where even kids tasked with baby-sitting their younger siblings are welcomed. At the Biblioteca Latinoamericana branch of the San Jose Public Library, adult volunteers conduct story times for toddlers while their older sisters and brothers receive homework assistance nearby. At another branch of the San Jose library, students are encouraged to make weekend appointments for homework help. Not only are public libraries open year-round, but they are also accessible during weekends and evenings. Where else can students find the information they need *when* they need it?

The Solution to Unattended Children

No one knows exactly how many kids nationwide visit their local public libraries after school. Of the 3,900 children who enter the County of Los Angeles Public Library between 2:00 and 5:00 P.M. everyday, 65 percent are unaccompanied by an adult and 20 percent are considered latchkey, that is, unattended. In public libraries across the country, staff use homework programs to help control otherwise-unsupervised mayhem. These programs may incorporate a combination of homework tasks and craft or story hours. At the Woodrow Wilson Community Library, in Fairfax County, Virginia, students from nearby elementary and middle schools occupy their afternoons by pairing up with volunteer tutors, who help them complete that day's homework. Once their homework is finished, the kids are then given a snack and educational games to play. A similar program, called Latchkey Enrichment, is so popular at the Queens Borough Public Library that several branches maintain lists of students waiting to enroll. According to staff, children who had previously presented disciplinary problems now are enthusiastically involved in library activities. Teachers also report improvement in students' reading ability.

By instituting formal after-school programs, librarians find that they can more readily focus their young patrons' energies on short-term projects, such as completing their homework. Rather than behaving in an unruly manner, the kids know they must exhibit constructive behavior if they are to continue participating in the library's after-school program. At the Woodrow Wilson Community Library, rules of conduct, including "No fighting" and "No running," are posted in the room where homework assistance is delivered. In East Palo Alto, California, inappropriate behavior earns kids demerits that may ultimately result in expulsion from the library's homework club. On the other hand, a consistent commitment to studying is rewarded through field trips to cultural and educational events. Likewise, at the Oakland Public Library's César E. Chávez branch, homework-center participants who demonstrate politeness and a willingness to help others are awarded a "Student of the Week" certificate and gift.

Librarians also find it much easier to discipline unattended children's conduct if the library provides a specific space for doing homework. At the Culver City Library, in California, the librarian notes a marked improvement in student behavior since the homework center was established. No matter how rowdy the kids are in other parts of the library, once they step through the center's archway they become serious students. The space itself defines the appropriate behaviors required to do homework, and so the library's rules of conduct are more easily enforced.

Benefits of Homework-Assistance Programs

The immediate benefits of children and young adults using their public libraries after school are apparent. While investigators recently established a connection between library use and higher standardized test scores, other emergent research directly links improved study habits and grades to after-school homework assistance. The key ingredient to better school performance, John P. Bailey surmised, after studying public library homework centers in Los Angeles County, was that students received personalized assistance from someone who had the time to explain directions and assignments and define vocabulary. In fact, 72 percent of the parents surveyed by Bailey indicated that their children came home with more complete schoolwork after attending the library's homework center. Elsewhere it was discovered that children read more as a result of their participation in the library's homework-assistance program and that math grades also improved.

Teachers also notice increased self-esteem in kids who receive homework help at the public library. In New Rochelle, New York, the library's after-school program, the Tall Tree Initiative, helps children grow scholastically and emotionally, inspiring a real can-do attitude. School librarian Bruce Seiden reports improved work quality among students and an increased desire to go to the library.

Students also learn how to cooperate with adults and each other by spending afternoons in their local public library. "I do my work on time and finish on time," boasted one Oakland fourth-grader, adding that he also does not "get mad or hit anybody" while at the library. At the Riverside Public Library's Cybrary, in California, staff provide basic behavior guidelines but allow the students to define their own after-school experience. While waiting to use the computers, Cybrary kids seek out activities and new responsibilities, such as being trained as tutor assistants, doing homework, and interacting positively with students from other schools they might never otherwise meet. Teamwork among the kids is also the key to success at A Place of Our Own, in Santa Cruz, California. There students learn from each other, exchanging hints on playing educational games, trading advice on word-processing software, and offering clues for creating wildly imaginative Web pages.

Library staff also notice improved English-language skills among their foreign-born patrons. In Castroville, California, homework-center staff work diligently with young Mexican immigrants to perfect new language skills. One student even completes assignments early so the homework helper can review her writing style and offer grammatical assistance. Likewise in Minneapolis, public library homework tutors have been instrumental in helping Somalian youngsters acclimate to their new home. "I couldn't speak a word of English when I came here three years ago," one young woman exclaimed. "And now look at me! I'll be going to college in the fall, thanks to the library!"

Another major benefit resulting from the library homework experience is the bond that often develops between the students and their mentors. Not only do kids bring to the library their school assignments, but they also share their real-life problems. At one library, tutors and students often discuss contemporary issues such as gang violence and drugs. Because they are of the same ethnicity and are not much older than the kids themselves, the tutors' advice is heeded. The homework helpers provide hope and encouragement in a neighborhood where few positive role models exist. In another example, mentors from a nearby university provide daily proof that succeeding in school is possible. For these students, going to college is now much less of an abstract idea and more of a concrete reality.

The kids are not the only ones who benefit from the various homework programs. At the Monterey Public Library, in California, one volunteer Homework Pal enthused that watching a child's scholastic abilities grow week after week can be a great joy. A second volunteer decided to pursue a master's degree in education as a result of being involved in the same program. Future teachers often play a critical role as homework facilitators. In Queens, for instance, two unattended-children program tutors regularly test the education concepts taught in their graduate courses; in Sacramento, one of the homework-center coordinators considers her daily work experience as a real-life "laboratory" for her master's thesis.

As for library staff, developing a broader service perspective is just one reward for being involved in after-school programs. Employees who initially doubted the appropriateness of such service in the library soon become converts when they see kids quietly doing their homework instead of causing unbridled havoc. One branch manager even credited the library's homework center with helping make her staff more culturally sensitive. Thanks to the richly diverse mixture of youngsters now using the facility after school, staff are less concerned with the students' racial or ethnic backgrounds than they are about meeting the kids' information needs.

Summary

Homework centers offer kids a designated place to go after school where they can get the scholastic support they need. Furthermore, unattended children are easier to discipline when the library provides a specific space for doing homework. Research has shown that children read more as a result of their participation in the library's homework-assistance program and that their math grades also improve. In addition, their self-esteem grows and they learn how to better cooperate with adults and other kids. English-language skills may also develop as a result of regularly using the library's homework center. Library staff and volunteers also gain from the homework experience, feeling joy at watching a student's skills grow and developing a broader service philosophy for themselves.

2

Needs Assessment

Following the first year of her library's successful After-School Study Center, youth-services officer Nancy Messineo observed that the foundation of any successful homework-assistance program is a solid needs assessment. Through surveys and interviews, staff at the Long Beach Public Library, in California, discovered that not only did recent Cambodian immigrants lack school supplies at home, but language barriers also prevented parents from helping their children complete class assignments. Thus originated the notion that the library could meet the much-neglected homework-assistance needs of its Cambodian community.

The need for a homework program is generally dictated by events either from within or outside the public library. In many cases, after-school homework centers are developed out of an internal need to manage chronically unruly patrons. Librarians in Seaside, California, Montclair, New Jersey, and Falls Church, Virginia, control the afternoon influx of unattended children by focusing their young wards' energies on homework and other creative tasks. Homework-assistance programs for older kids, however, tend to be more motivated by societal or external forces. The Riverside County Library, in California, established its homework program as a preventive measure against behavior exhibited in the 1992 Los Angeles riots. The teen homework center in Austin, Texas, was instigated in response to a critical school-dropout rate.

Before launching any new program, librarians find that it is best to first assess their constituents' need for such a service. In so doing, existent services and unmet needs are identified, providing a basis for resetting the library's priorities. If done correctly, the needs assessment also awakens community awareness and hopefully encourages other local organizations to collaborate with the library in tackling the issues identified.

Involving the Community

Because public library service should directly reflect the target population's needs, the most successful homework-assistance programs are those born out of the community's desire for such a service. In San Bernardino County, California, the library's Family Technology Learning Center (TLC) was created as a result of a three-day strategic-planning process initiated by a team of community leaders who solicited input from two school districts and various focus groups. The Family TLC was started to meet the specific needs outlined in the team's strategy to "support and develop existing and new life skills programs." Responding to this mandate, Family TLC staff currently provide computer access and training, bilingual services and materials, extended library hours, and homework resources.

In a similar process, the Hennepin County Library, in Minnesota, sponsored a two-day Future Search Conference to help the library envision programs to meet the needs of its several communities. As a result of expressed concerns over the gap between the information "haves" and "have-nots," Hennepin County developed the KidLinks program to provide electronic homework and information resources for youngsters.

To ensure that the library's constituents are included in the homework-center planning process, many librarians recruit an advisory team made up of community members interested in youth-related matters. At the Wallace Branch of the East Central Georgia Regional Library, staff have established a "homework council" composed of parents, board of education personnel, teachers, library board members, and several high-school students. This group acts as a steering committee that helps the library plan the homework-center's goals, policies, programs, and any needed changes. Such a group may also prove instrumental in developing a relevant method for assessing community need. The Corvallis–Benton County Public Library, in Oregon, formed a student advisory council to help create a questionnaire to query students and teachers about homework needs. Not only did the advisory council's input guarantee a well-crafted survey, but their involvement in the process maximized good public relations.

Assessment Methods

Stan Weisner, former director of the Bay Area Youth at Risk Project, recommends a three-pronged approach to assessing community needs. To complete as thorough an assessment as possible, library staff must

1. review the existent literature,
2. observe the situation firsthand, and
3. conduct a survey.

The first of these three tasks—collecting "secondary data" through a literature search—should, of course, come quite naturally for librarians. Local area demographics and descriptions of existing youth services are basic bits of information available at most public libraries. In addition, librarians usually have easy access to relevant periodical articles and reports generated by other community agencies. The findings of a citizens' panel on youth and violence, for example, proved particularly helpful when librarians in Fort Wayne, Indiana, began planning their after-school homework program for teens. The panel's conclusion that youth do not receive much homework assistance outside the library substantiated staff's own observations on the matter. The citizens' report also validated the library's need for increased funding.

The second step in the assessment process is firsthand observation. Staff can certainly attest to the fact that the library is inundated every day with young patrons needing homework help. Still, not all homework activity goes on exclusively inside the library. Whenever possible, librarians should make a point of observing kids in their natural settings. In Chicago, public library staff made "outreach visits" into the high schools and parks, where they learned that kids primarily needed a place to study away from siblings. Librarians should consider visiting schools, youth-service agencies, after-school recreation programs, and public-housing projects to view their young constituents up close. Such qualitative data will prove invaluable when interpreting survey results and other quantitative information collected.

The main purpose of a survey—the third step in the assessment process—is to collect information about the opinions, attitudes, and beliefs of a representative group of individuals about a particular issue. After observing thousands of kids coming to the Brooklyn Public Library for homework help, librarian Barbara Auerbach decided to query them as to exactly what type of homework assistance they needed. When 84 percent of the kids surveyed indicated a need for math help, the library decided to offer a Math Peer Tutoring program.

Surveys are usually conducted as questionnaires or interviews and are relatively inexpensive to administer. When developing the survey instrument, the assessment committee must first decide exactly what information is required to assess the community's needs. Surveys should be brief, free of technical jargon, and written to the respondent's level of knowledge (*see* appendix B for examples). Questionnaires should also be easy to return either via the mail or to a box located inside the library.

Faced with eliminating programs at the Garfield Park Branch, administrators of the public library in Santa Cruz, California, decided to ask their young patrons which services the branch should offer. Every person participating in the survey indicated a need to access technology at the library. Eighty-eight percent also said they used the library for homework support. Prompted by these and other findings, the installation of electronic resources became the branch's top priority as an after-school program, called A Place of Our Own, was launched.

In Fort Wayne, the library conducted a study to determine the feasibility of a homework-help center for teens. Questionnaires were mailed to young adult summer reading club participants and were distributed at schools, youth centers, and inside the library. More than nine hundred responses were collected. Of these, 81 percent indicated a need for homework assistance, with 56 percent saying they would use a homework-help program at the library if offered. When asked what times would be most convenient for them to come to the library, 44 percent responded that after school would be best, while 39 percent preferred evenings. Armed with these data, library staff then interviewed representatives from local homework-support agencies to determine a possible overlap in programs. They also led a focus-group discussion with twenty-two teens. Information solicited here included ways to market a library homework program to kids. The data collected in all three surveys not only helped staff shape the homework center, but also convinced funders of the need. Today, homework assistance is provided three nights a week at the Allen County Public Library in Fort Wayne.

The assessment process may also be used to measure the need for an expanded program. For six years, the Oakland Public Library has provided homework assistance to children through its highly effective PASS! (Partners for Achieving School Success) program. The library is now looking to expand services to young adults. To ensure that the new program is relevant to their needs, teen input was solicited through two focus groups and a survey. The investigators found that although less than half of the kids surveyed currently use the library for homework assistance, 74 percent would use a formal homework-help program if offered by the library. Not surprisingly, providing a formal homework-assistance program is among the top recommendations for expanding library services to teens.

Summary

Although public librarians may be motivated by several different factors to offer homework-assistance service, the most successful programs are the ones developed to meet the community's specific homework needs. To fully appreciate the public's need for homework assistance, library staff must include community members in the service planning process. Staff should also assess needs through a search of the existent literature, firsthand observation, and survey techniques.

3 Service Plan

Because each program reflects the needs of its particular community, no two homework centers are exactly alike. Even within the same library system, programs may differ from branch to branch because of specific circumstances and individual community needs. Therefore, a written plan is necessary to distinguish exactly what role the library plays as a homework-assistance provider.

Defining the Program

Many public libraries incorporate into their mission statements a promise to meet the "educational needs" of the community. Before launching a homework-assistance program, staff and administrators must first revisit the library's mission to ensure that meeting their constituents' curricular needs is indeed part of the library's overall service plan. If not, then the proposed program either lies outside the library's parameters or may represent a neglected need of the community. In the latter case, a needs-assessment survey would help clarify the possible necessity for resetting the library's priorities.

The most successful homework-assistance programs are those based on a mission statement that commits the library to meeting the learning and educational needs of its community. The mission of Baltimore's Enoch Pratt Free Library, for instance, is "to provide access to information resources, staff, facilities, and services that respond to the pursuit of knowledge, education, lifelong learning opportunities, and cultural enrichment." Likewise, the mission of the County of Los Angeles Public Library is to provide "a network of community-focused libraries that meet the informational, educational and recreational needs of a highly diverse public." In Minneapolis not only is the public library considered an educational resource "for the people of the community," but the library's first two stated

10

purposes are to "open doors to learning for children" and "assist students of all ages." The emphasis on *education* in all of these statements indicates a commitment to meeting the curricular needs of the community and lays a foundation for building after-school homework-assistance programs. But such a commitment must first be present in the library's mission statement if the homework center is to succeed.

From the mission statement come the library's goals, objectives, and definitions of service. If curricular support is to be fully integrated into the library's services, then a policy for achieving such a goal must be included in the library's work plan. Several libraries have developed homework-assistance programs by first defining exactly what that service entails. In Los Angeles County, a "Homework Help Center" is very specifically defined as a "library based after-school service designed to provide supervised homework assistance; an enhanced collection of homework support materials; computer-based learning opportunities; enrichment opportunities in subjects such as science, math, literature or the arts; enhancement of study skills; and development of parent support materials." Although branch staff are given latitude on how to accomplish these goals, program expectations are clear. In addition, a written procedures manual provides guidance in all decision making related to the Homework Help Centers.

Once the service parameters of the program are defined, a specific plan for achieving them can be developed. The most effective homework programs are those managed by objectives that detail student-recruitment methods, expected academic outcomes, requisite resources, necessary partnerships, and overall benefits. Often these objectives are outlined in grant applications or other management documents (*see* appendix C) and are frequently used to measure the success of the program.

In a proposed pilot project that was eventually adopted by the Sacramento Public Library, homework-center staff outlined their strategy to enroll one hundred at-risk youth into an after-school program. The goal of improving academic performance was to be achieved through structured orientation to the library and through peer support among program participants during weekly group activities. To accomplish the overall goal of strengthening after-school use of the library, personal computers were installed with interactive software and Internet access. As a final objective, carefully orchestrated partnerships with parents and teachers from three nearby schools were built into the program to ensure student support.

In East Palo Alto, California, librarians maintain a regular core of twenty at-risk student participants identified through referrals from teachers and social service workers. Staff also strive to attract a monthly average of fifty drop-in teens through publicity to the general public. In addition, youth needing help with reading and/or English-language skills receive special tutoring. Other program objectives include recruiting volunteer homework assistants from area businesses, corporations, and Stanford University student organizations; soliciting donations from businesses for needed school supplies; and purchasing materials to fill gaps in the collection.

Both the Sacramento and East Palo Alto program objectives are well thought out and specific, giving staff a solid plan for providing effective homework assistance. These objectives are also used to measure the success of the program at year's end.

Responsibility for Carrying Out the Program

Either before or directly after the planning process, responsibility for running the homework program must be assigned. For the most part, after-school homework centers are administered by the children's and/or young adult services librarian, depending on the age of the students served. Because answering homework questions and providing after-school programs for kids are traditionally handled by the youth services librarians, coordination of any formal homework-assistance program most often becomes part of their purview. In fact, the idea for providing such a service may be initially suggested by the children's or young adult librarian, especially if there is a perceived need to control unattended children after school. In the small town of Northfield, Minnesota, for instance, the youth services librarians noticed that local kids had little to do after school. Thus was born the Homework Cafe, which the librarians themselves run with the help of volunteers. The librarians schedule and physically set up the library's community room, where the Cafe is held every week. They also recruit and "hire" the homework assistants and generate all program publicity.

In large public libraries, such as Los Angeles County, Minneapolis, and Queens, the youth services coordinator typically oversees the librarywide program, while branch staff are responsible for the individual homework center's day-to-day operation. This configuration allows for a consistent homework policy throughout the library while encouraging flexibility at the local level. At the San Jose Public Library, for example, branch managers are responsible for allocating and spending their own local homework-center budgets, even though the program as a whole is administered by the librarywide youth services coordinator.

Although all homework-assistance programs serve teens or younger students, not all of them are administered by youth services librarians. Orange Public Library's Friendly Stop homework center, in California, was considered a satellite branch of the central library and so was managed by the director of that facility. In Riverside, California, the freestanding Cybrary, which is open primarily for students after school and on Saturdays, is run as a branch library. Rather than a children's or young adult services librarian, the Cybrary is supervised by a project manager who reports to an administrator within the larger organization.

In some libraries, the purpose of the homework center aligns more closely with the goals of departments other than youth services. For instance, Multnomah County Library's Homework Helper program, in Oregon, is considered an extension of reference service. The Homework Helpers, who report to the volunteer-services coordinator, are trained to assist students of all ages. In Corona, California, the library's after-school homework center is run by literacy staff, who early on realized a need to serve the children of parents enrolled in the library's literacy program. Currently some fourteen children a day receive help with their school assignments, while their parents learn to read in another part of the library. In South San Francisco, the library's Community Learning Center (CLC) offers homework assistance to first- through fifth-graders as part of an overall education agenda that includes teaching English as a second language and helping adults acquire computer skills. Like the homework program in Corona, the CLC is administered by the literacy department.

A few libraries outsource their homework services, preferring to delegate the management of the program to an outside agency. At the Monroe County Public Library, in Indiana, homework assistance to children is coordinated by a federally funded Americorps employee, who hires, trains, and schedules a battery of "coaches" to help kids hone their reading skills and complete homework. Although the homework tutoring actually occurs in the library, the program is considered part of the statewide Indiana Reading Team and is administered separately from the library's own math-assistance program. In Ventura County, California, homework help, called SchooLinks, is both funded and managed by the Ojai Valley Library Foundation. Not only is SchooLinks a part of the after-school service offered at every public library branch in Ojai Valley, but the ultimate goal is to incorporate the program into every school there as well. The advantage of having an outside agency, rather than the library, coordinate this multidepartmental effort is apparent. Furthermore, because SchooLinks is privately funded, the program has been able to flourish even during lean economic times and, in fact, is credited with providing the Ojai Valley branches with equipment and materials the library could not otherwise afford.

Summary

A written plan is necessary to distinguish exactly what role the library plays as a homework-assistance provider. This plan should reflect the library's mission to provide curricular support to its community and should include succinct objectives for attaining that goal. Either before or directly after the planning process, responsibility for running the home-work program must be assigned. Although many after-school homework centers are administered by the children's and/or young adult services librarian, some are run by other library departments, depending on the goals of the particular homework program. Managing the homework center may also be delegated to an outside agency, such as Americorps or the library's foundation, if appropriate to the library's structure.

4

Staff and Volunteeer Recruitment

P roviding adequate staff is the single most-important element to developing an effective homework-assistance program. Although some librarians may call their curriculum-based collection of computers and reference materials a homework *center*, true homework *assistance* cannot occur without a staff member or volunteers helping students complete their work. Research has shown that youngsters often need adult or peer attention to help keep them on task when completing their school assignments. Many of them also need validation to succeed. As the Carnegie Council on Adolescent Development reported in 1995, 98 percent of students do better in school when they work with a trained tutor.

The challenge, of course, comes in maintaining a paid or volunteer workforce large enough to provide sufficient assistance to the multitude of students who use the library every day after school. Most libraries cannot afford to hire the number of part-time employees needed to help kids with their homework. Nor are they prepared to recruit and train a battery of after-school volunteers. Yet many libraries have succeeded in accomplishing the seemingly impossible task of providing one-on-one homework assistance to their young patrons by utilizing paid and volunteer staff to their maximum.

Paid versus Volunteer Staff

According to a 1999 American Library Association survey, more than 50 percent of the public libraries that provide formal homework assistance do so with volunteer help. Indeed, some of the most successful programs are those that use volunteer homework assistants. An outstanding example is the Monterey Public Library, in California, which utilizes some fifty volunteer Homework Pals a year. Although library staff are responsible for recruiting, training, and scheduling the volunteers, the Pals themselves provide direct homework assistance to elementary-school children. Most of these volunteers are motivated by a desire to work with kids (e.g., seniors whose grandchildren have moved across the country, a prison worker who needs a positive change of pace, and college students studying to be teachers). As compensation, the volunteers are given free library cards and are treated as part of the staff; but for most Pals, their biggest reward is in helping children learn.

Another fine example of a mostly volunteer-run homework program is the Northfield Public Library's Homework Cafe, in Minnesota. The youth-services librarians arrange for the facility and advertise the service, but a team of unpaid college students actually provides the after-school homework assistance. In addition, one of the volunteers is responsible for scheduling and communicating with all the others, freeing the librarians to work on more-pressing demands. The homework helpers are rewarded through staff letters of recommendation and gift certificates to local campus bookstores and bagel shops. This rather low-budget operation succeeds, in large part, thanks to staff ingenuity and creative delegation.

In lieu of a salary, many volunteer homework assistants are given free parking passes, free e-mail accounts, T-shirts, lapel pins, mugs, water bottles, and lots of recognition through their library's newsletter and special functions like the annual Volunteer Tea. Still, because they are unpaid, not all volunteers are completely reliable. This is especially true of college or high-school students, who graduate or leave for paying jobs. In a program where familiarity breeds trust and commitment, consistency of service is imperative. Therefore, some libraries make a priority of paying their homework helpers.

The Queens Borough Public Library has found paid staff to be much more dependable and so hires its homework monitors for the school year. At the County of Los Angeles Public Library, homework helpers are hired year-round, working as library pages when school is out. Because the homework-center staff are paid employees, library managers feel comfortable asking them to keep records and written reports of the program's progress. In addition, because the library hires its homework staff from the surrounding community, these people also serve as positive role models.

Rosellen Brewer, of the Monterey County Free Libraries, suggests that a combination of paid and volunteer staff be used to maximize resources. In Monterey County, a part-time homework-site coordinator is hired to oversee each local program and recruit and schedule volunteer assistants. At the Castroville branch, for instance, the site coordinator works closely with the local university to recruit "service learning" students, who are required to contribute thirty hours per semester to community agencies. She also works with various local organizations to solicit donated computer equipment for the homework center. This model of hiring part-time site coordinators is also effectively used at the San Jose, Oakland, and Monroe County, Indiana, public libraries.

Staff Qualifications

Regardless of whether staff are paid or not, most libraries desire very specific qualities and skills in their homework helpers and site coordinators. Above all else, homework staff must enjoy working with kids and possess a commitment to education. Knowledge and experience with computers may also be required. At the Venice Beach branch of the Los Angeles

Public Library, homework-center staff are responsible for maintaining computer hardware, monitoring equipment use, responding to troubleshooting questions, and providing one-on-one as well as group training. Homework assistants everywhere must also have good communication skills and, in at least one library, must be able to read aloud "expressively." Math ability is desirable and is even tested as part of the interview process in some libraries. In places like Tucson and Oakland, Sacramento, and Long Beach, California, bilingualism in a variety of languages is also required of homework helpers. Other more generic qualifications include demonstrated problem-solving skills, patience, organizational skills, flexibility, the ability to work as a team player, access to reliable transportation, and availability after school.

Previous experience working with youth, either in a paid or voluntary capacity, is also highly desirable. In particular, libraries consider former or future librarians and teachers to be well-qualified homework-help candidates. Several public libraries, including those in Yonkers, San Jose, and Monroe County, make excellent use of practicing educators who are hired to work in the library after school. In New Rochelle, New York, the Teacher in the Library program has gone a long way toward strengthening relations between the public library and local schools. The children benefit from working with familiar and well-respected mentors; plus, when assignments seem unreasonable, the teachers use their contacts to let colleagues know the library's limitations.

Recruitment

Homework assistants are generally recruited in the fall, before the school year begins. Various libraries use different methods of recruitment, including sponsoring announcements on the radio and television or in community calendars and agency newsletters. Ads are also placed in the newspaper, and flyers are posted in and outside the library (*see* appendix D for examples). In the small town of Montclair, California, homework staff secure volunteers by chatting with people in the library and by visiting the local computer store. The coordinator of volunteer services for the Allen County Public Library, in Indiana, sends an annual letter to local agencies and businesses, requesting their help in promoting the library's homework program. Among the most responsive groups are the professional engineering associations, which encourage their members to become homework helpers.

Several libraries make good use of established programs such as Literacy Volunteers of America (LVA), Volunteers in Service to America (VISTA), Reserve Officers Training Corps (ROTC), America Reads, the Learning Is ForEver Society (LIFE), and the Retired Senior Volunteer Program (RSVP). In San Diego County, librarians have teamed up with law enforcement officers to bring curriculum support and positive role models into the library. This is accomplished through STAR/PAL (Sports Training, Academics and Recreation/Police Athletic League), a program that places uniformed personnel in the library after school specifically to assist kids with their homework. Not only do the students receive help with their assignments, but they gain a new respect for the officers they might otherwise distrust.

Other rich sources for recruiting homework assistants are colleges and local high schools. Because volunteer library work often meets curriculum service requisites, recruiting older students as homework helpers benefits both the library and the volunteers. In addition, because homework centers are open after school, students can commit their time without missing class. Helpers are secured through school volunteer fairs and direct contact with school officials. In National City, California, prospective tutors were recruited through the high school's peer counseling teacher. In Brooklyn, local mathematics teachers refer teenaged math tutors.

College-aged tutors not only bring with them valued subject expertise, but they also provide younger kids with powerful role models, especially in communities where dropout rates are high. Education majors and members of Future Teachers of America work particularly well with younger kids. Oftentimes older students treat the homework center as a laboratory for testing their own teaching and disciplinary skills. At one library, the homework-site coordinator plans to use her daily experience as the basis for her master's thesis. At another, the homework assistant decided to become an education major as a direct result of working with kids everyday.

Besides college-aged tutors, librarians also welcome the help of teenaged homework assistants. Despite some minor problems with teen tutors forming cliques or flirting with peers, librarians have found that high-school-aged homework helpers perform as well, if not better than, their older counterparts. In Oakland, the use of teenaged mentors is an integral part of the PASS! program's success. Here honor students are hired by the Youth Employment Partnership, which then places them in the library as after-school homework assistants. The high schoolers not only gain a sense of pride from serving the community, but their own learning is reinforced as they help others study. Teen tutors tend to become more socially competent and are better prepared for the job market as a result of their homework-center experience. The teens' young protégés benefit as well. In Jasper, Tennessee, the number of children considered "at risk" dropped by 70 percent after the public library initiated a Young Adult Reading Council composed of some thirty middle- and high-school students who help the younger kids with their schoolwork.

The Hiring Process

Whether or not they are paid employees, most prospective homework helpers undergo a hiring process once they are recruited into the library's program. In many cases, this process includes an application form and interview and may even include an examination to test for English comprehension or math skills or both.

Along with name, address, and telephone number, most application forms request information about prior work and volunteer experience and educational background (*see* appendix E for sample application forms). The library may also ask if the applicant has any special skills, such as experience in leading story times, reading one-on-one, and coordinating art projects, or if the applicant has knowledge of math and languages other than

English. The names of one or two references are usually required, as are the name and telephone number of an emergency contact. Applicants are also asked why they wish to volunteer or become a homework helper and what times and days of the week they are available. Finally, most libraries want to know if prospective tutors and homework-site coordinators have been convicted of a crime.

The applicants' qualifications may be further scrutinized during an interview, where candidates are asked to describe everything from their overall career goals to details about past experiences working with children. Typical homework-helper interview questions may include the following:

- Why do you think you would be an effective homework helper?

- What do you think is the most important benefit we offer the students?

- A student you are working with gets upset and can't understand what you are trying to explain. Finally, the student tells you that you are not very good at explaining things at all. What would you say or do?

- How would you deal with children who don't want to be at the homework center but whose parents insist that they be there?

- How would you go about developing the reading skills of a student who has difficulty reading?

- How would you gauge a student's improved reading performance or knowledge of a particular subject?

- How would you attract students to the homework center?

- What are some ways you can motivate students to learn?

- In your past tutoring experience, have you ever had a situation where you could not help a student? What was the situation? What were the methods you used to try to reach the student?

- What subject areas do you feel you have expertise in or are less familiar with? How would you help a student in those areas?

- Tell us about your experience helping a student with a research project. Tell us how you approached it. If you have not helped a student with research, tell us how you approached your own project.

- You may have several students needing help at the same time. How would you proceed?

Interviews with prospective homework-site coordinators may also include in-depth queries on how the person would gain stakeholder support and how to measure program effectiveness. Role-playing may also be included as part of the interview process.

After volunteer applicants pass the interview and agree to become part of the homework-center staff, they then may be asked to sign a contract specifying duties and expectations (*see* appendix F for sample forms). Generally, these contracts spell out a mutual working agreement and direct the volunteers to immediately notify library staff in case of absence.

Libraries may also use the contract to outline restrictions regarding physical contact with children, meeting young patrons outside the library, and initiating discussions of a controversial nature.

In addition to signing a contract, volunteers may also be subjected to a security check and asked for fingerprints. At the Monterey Public Library, all Homework Pals are tested for tuberculosis as part of the school district's staff requirements.

Summary

Providing adequate staff is the single most-important element to developing an effective homework-assistance program. Because youngsters often need adult or peer attention to help keep them on task, true homework assistance cannot occur without a staff member or volunteers helping students complete their work. Although 50 percent of all homework programs utilize volunteer helpers, some libraries have found paid staff to be more reliable. Regardless of whether helpers are paid or not, libraries require very specific qualities and skills in their homework staff, including an ability and desire to work with kids and a commitment to education. Former or future librarians and teachers are particularly desirable as homework helpers as they often provide valuable links to local schools. Other well-qualified volunteers include college and high-school students. Whether or not they are paid employees, most prospective homework helpers undergo a hiring process once they are recruited into the library's program. In many cases, this process includes an application form and interview and may even include an examination to test for English comprehension and math skills.

5

Job Duties and Training

To distinguish among the roles of the various homework-center staff, many libraries have developed job descriptions for both paid and volunteer workers (*see* appendix G for examples). Such job descriptions not only help to identify the differences between the homework-mentor and site-coordinator positions, but they also describe what makes homework-center staff distinct from other library employees.

For the most part, homework-center staff are unique in that they are specifically trained to work directly and exclusively with students. Although other library staff may help students by providing materials and information to answer homework questions, homework-center staff take a more proactive role by advising kids how to proceed with their schoolwork. Depending on the library, homework helpers may review student assignments, explain instructions, check student work, drill youngsters in math and spelling, help prepare for tests, and even strengthen the child's reading skills. Their main task is to ensure student success by providing the necessary tools and encouragement to enable kids to complete their own homework.

Job Duties

Homework-center employees and volunteers may be called any one of a number of different titles. In Monterey, California, these people are referred to as "Homework Pals"; in Oakland, they are called "mentors." Regardless of whether they are known as homework "tutors," "coaches," "assistants," or "helpers," their job duties generally range from assisting kids with schoolwork to keeping daily statistics. Tasks may include

- creating a neat and welcoming atmosphere,
- registering students and/or maintaining a daily log of homework-center use,
- setting up homework-center materials and supplies,

- helping students complete homework assignments,
- developing supplementary learning materials,
- referring complicated research questions to the librarian,
- training and supervising kids in the use of the library's computers,
- serving as a mentor by listening and talking with students about current issues and by modeling positive values,
- ensuring that students adhere to library rules of behavior,
- acting as a liaison between the library and teachers to clarify assignments,
- promoting the homework-center program through outreach and publicity,
- assisting in the program-evaluation process, and
- assisting staff in daily library operations.

To control turnover as much as possible, volunteer helpers usually agree to work at least two hours a week. Many libraries also require their homework-center staff to make a long-term service commitment of at least four months or an entire school semester.

Besides homework helpers, some libraries also use supervisory staff to run the homework program. These staff members are often called site or program "coordinators" or "lead" homework tutors or assistants. Their duties may include

- maintaining a generally positive learning atmosphere,
- scheduling and training homework helpers,
- helping students complete homework assignments,
- developing supplementary learning materials,
- conducting regular staff meetings with homework helpers,
- planning and presenting group programs for students and/or parents,
- collaborating with library staff to carry out the goals of the program,
- maintaining program records and submitting reports,
- ordering supplies as needed, and
- working closely with parents and teachers to publicize the program and check on students' progress.

Because of their level of responsibility, site coordinators tend to be part-time paid employees who work only during homework-center hours.

Training

Before paid and volunteer staff can implement the tasks outlined in a job description, they need to be trained. It comes as no surprise, therefore, that the most effective after-school homework programs are those that make a priority of training new and continuing staff. At the Cybrary, in Riverside, California, all tutors undergo extensive training before they are allowed to train students how to use the library's computers. Based on the Enoch Pratt Free Library's Whole New World training model, in Baltimore, Cybrary staff developed an extensive manual that guides tutors through detailed use of the library's computer equipment and software. Included are exercises for becoming familiar with the keyboard and mouse, instructions for setting up e-mail accounts and Web pages, and numerous opportunities for practicing word processing and Internet searching. Once the training is completed, the tutor is given a superhighway "driving exam" and, if successful, is then awarded a Cybrary "license" to work with kids after school.

In Multnomah County, Oregon, initial homework-helper training occurs over three days during the fall. At the first meeting, volunteers are introduced to general intellectual-freedom concepts, as well as the library's online catalog and magazine database. A week later, they are taught how to use the Internet and how to conduct a reference interview. This is followed by a review session several weeks later. In addition, all homework-help volunteers are required to shadow a library staff member to see how that person works with students. The volunteers' interaction with the public is then observed before they are released to work on their own. A similar orientation has been instituted at the Educational Park Branch of Sacramento Public Library, where all homework assistants spend a week "in training" before doing any actual tutoring. During this period, they familiarize themselves with staff and the students while learning the importance of the mentoring process.

One or several different staff members may conduct the homework-center training depending on the structure and goals of the program. At the Monterey Public Library, the Homework Pals coordinator and youth-services manager work together to present a thorough all-day orientation. In Allen County, Indiana, the young adult librarian and volunteer-services coordinator do most of the training. Administrators of larger organizations may present a broader librarywide overview, leaving operational details to be explained by the branch manager or site coordinator. Homework-helper training may even be partially outsourced. In San Bernardino County, for example, volunteer computer training is handled by local school personnel through the California Technology Assistance Project; in Oakland, the Youth Employment Partnership teaches prospective homework mentors basic work ethics and skills.

Whether it is conducted "on the spot" or through well-organized sessions, orientation of homework-center staff should include a combination of the following:

- an overview of the library's mission and the role of the homework center;
- a commitment to promoting a positive and safe learning environment;
- a description of program policies, procedures, and performance expectations;
- copies of pertinent forms and schedules;
- an introduction to the library's resources and how to use them;
- hands-on practice using library technology;
- techniques for working with students;
- an explanation of when reference questions should be referred to the librarian;

- sensitivity to cultural and ethnic diversity; and
- a tour of the facility.

In some libraries, helpers are given practice homework questions that they then have to answer as part of the training process. These questions not only test ability at using the library's resources, but also expose staff to the wide range of queries they may encounter after school. Examples from the Multnomah County Library follow:

- Can you help me find a book about dinosaurs?
- I need a book on Greek mythology.
- We're studying the Oregon Trail, and I have to find out what people ate when they were on the trail. Can you help me?
- Do you have any videos about Kwanzaa?
- I need to find a biography of a famous explorer.
- I am writing a one-page report on cocaine and need an article with general information.
- I need an overview of tuberculosis for my health-class report, but it can't be from a book or encyclopedia.
- Are there any recent civil rights controversies in Australia?
- I need an interview with Maurice Sendak, but I can't use *Something about the Author*.
- How do I build a volcano that erupts?

Initial training is often reinforced during refresher workshops held throughout the school year. In Minneapolis, school officials offer library staff free training sessions on math homework, privacy issues, and how to communicate effectively with parents and teachers. Likewise, in Monterey, teachers and other experts have conducted workshops on learning disabilities, learning methods, and how to develop math and English-language skills. Requests for training on specific topics are generated by the Homework Pals, with whom the program coordinator meets regularly.

Summary

Job descriptions are necessary to identify the differences between the homework-mentor and site-coordinator positions, as well as to describe the tasks and qualifications that make homework-center staff distinct from other library employees. Although other library staff primarily help students by providing materials and information to answer homework questions, homework-center staff take a more proactive role by advising kids how to proceed with their schoolwork. The main task of homework-help staff is to ensure student success by providing the necessary tools and encouragement to enable kids to complete their own work. Training and follow-up workshops help staff implement the tasks outlined in the job description.

6

Funding and Partnerships

Although some programs, like Northfield's Homework Cafe, in Minnesota, and Brooklyn's Math Peer Tutoring, are funded through the library's regular budget, most after-school homework centers exist solely thanks to outside-funding sources. Occasionally, programs that began as grant-funded projects, such as the Tall Tree Initiative in New Rochelle, New York, and Fairfax County's homework-help center, in Virginia, become fully integrated into the library's budget. For the most part, however, acquiring the resources to adequately staff and equip the homework center is an ongoing exercise that continually tests librarians' fund-raising and community-relations skills.

Funding Sources

Extremely helpful in generating funds for after-school homework programs are library foundations that have made educational or youth services a top priority. Often acting as the homework-center's fiscal agent, the library foundation can, as a nonprofit entity, apply for grants and other funding opportunities not usually made available to government agencies. The Library Foundation of Los Angeles, for instance, has successfully solicited support from the J. Paul Getty Trust, MCA/Universal Studios, Toyota Motor Sales, Sanwa Bank California, and the Samuel Goldwyn Foundation to continue Los Angeles Public Library's multibranch after-school homework-assistance program. In Ventura County, California, the Ojai Valley Library Foundation subsidizes the library's SchooLinks program through grants and donations from various local businesses and organizations.

In recent years, libraries have begun to rely on the munificence of private funders to financially support what some consider "value-added" services. Not only do these funders tend to share the library's commitment to educational or cultural endeavors, but they also care about the welfare of their communities. Particularly generous are financial institutions and local industries that regularly support all types of after-school programs. A notable example is the rail transportation carrier Conrail, which has a reputation of being a good neighbor in communities where it maintains facilities. In Toledo, Ohio, Conrail provides assistance to seven branch-library homework centers.

Another good friend to public libraries is the Wells Fargo Bank, which donated the seed money for several homework-help centers in San Diego County, as well as $50,000 to the Multnomah County Library to pay for the second year of its homework-assistance program. Other supportive financial institutions include the Bank of America Foundation, which gave the Dallas Public Library $35,000, and Putnam Investments, which contributed $100,000 to initiate Boston Public Library's Schiebler Homework Assistance Program. In Ventura County, the First Interstate Bank of California's foundation underwrote staffing costs to establish and run the library's first homework-center site.

Locally based corporations may also be very supportive of the library's educational efforts. In the Los Angeles area, the entertainment industry has been instrumental in developing several homework-assistance programs. Sony Pictures donated $50,000 in computer equipment and furnishings to help launch the county library's homework center in Culver City. Likewise, the CBS Foundation contributed more than $175,000 to install up-to-date computer equipment in a number of Los Angeles Public Library's after-school homework sites. Local oil companies have also been big contributors to homework programs in California and Texas, with Unocal, Chevron, Conoco, and ARCO all donating money for library technology.

Computer companies have also become natural partners in the establishment of homework programs. Seattle Public Library's After School Happenings (SPLASH) is a direct result of Microsoft's Libraries Online! gift program, which equipped a low-income community branch library with five networked computers. Elsewhere, the Homework Alert Centers at the Corvallis–Benton County Public Library, in Oregon, were made possible, in large part, through a major contribution of computer equipment by Hewlett-Packard. By aligning themselves with after-school library programs, these and other corporations not only meet their own institutional goals, but also become identified with service providers that help youth of all ages. The corporate sponsor improves its public relations image while upgrading the library's service to its community.

Another major source of homework-center funding is the federal government, which, through the Library Services and Technology Act (LSTA), has provided the start-up money for many after-school homework programs throughout the country. Libraries in California, New York, and Massachusetts have taken particularly good advantage of these federal funding opportunities. In most states, LSTA monies are administered through the state library, which awards grants on an annual, competitive basis. Unfortunately, because LSTA funds are typically earmarked for pilot projects that demonstrate new library services, these monies cannot be used to support a program longer than one or two years. Still, several model homework programs might not exist if not for LSTA support. Examples of successful federally funded homework-assistance projects include San Bernardino County Library's Family Technology Learning Center (TLC), Riverside Public Library's Cybrary, Santa Cruz City-County Public Library's A Place of Our Own, and Queens Borough Public Library's

Latchkey Enrichment Program. In Massachusetts, the State Board of Library Commissioners issues $6,000 LSTA-funded homework-center minigrants to libraries serving populations of less than fifteen-thousand people. Federal money is also used to sponsor homework-assistance training, program publicity, and a staff manual.

Another source of federal funding is Community Development Block Grants (CDBGs), which are usually administered at the city and county levels. CDBG awards generally target low-income and blighted neighborhoods in dire need of improved local service. Depending on the jurisdiction, these funds may be used for providing enhanced facilities and/or hiring staff. In Orange, the Friendly Stop, which was located in a Latino barrio, was able to stay open two years beyond its initial funding thanks to a CDBG. At the New Rochelle Public Library, CDBG funds are used to hire bilingual homework assistants, who also provide service to the library's satellite homework center located in a local housing project.

In addition to federal funding, states and local governing bodies may also support public library homework efforts through various grant opportunities. In Minnesota, for instance, both the Minneapolis and Hennepin County libraries have received State Department of Children, Families and Learning "technology enhancement" grants to bring enriched after-school homework assistance to their respective communities. Elsewhere, public libraries may be eligible for local funds aimed at preventing crime and reducing juvenile delinquency. The East Palo Alto Library's Quest homework center, which is now fully funded by the library, was originally financed through San Mateo County's "prevention program" budget. Likewise, San Diego Public Library's homework centers were initially funded through the city's Neighborhood Pride and Protection program, which targeted communities plagued with substance abuse and gang and criminal activity. As these examples demonstrate, librarians may successfully compete for "prevention" funds if they can convince local officials that homework-assistance services help reduce risks to kids after school. (For samples of grant proposals, *see* appendix H.)

Community Partnerships

Although not all homework-assistance programs require huge sums of money to get started, all of them do require a commitment from the community they serve. Not only do the library's constituents help define the need for a homework center, in many cases they may also be asked to provide a source of support for continuing the program. Indeed, most public library homework centers benefit directly from the generosity of their communities. Once library staff successfully create partnerships with local organizations and businesses, gifts of equipment, money, or volunteer services often soon follow.

Good partners to have in promoting all library programs are sibling city and county departments. They, too, often seek cooperative partners and may add a unique dimension to the library's homework-assistance program. In Ventura County, for example, a partnership between the library and the city of Ojai has enabled SchooLinks participants to receive free intercity trolley rides to and from the library's homework centers.

Over the years, librarians have developed particularly good working relationships with parks and recreation personnel, who tend to share some of the same service goals as the public library. In 1990, the Seattle Public Library and the Department of Parks and Recreation teamed up to create KEY/HELP, a cooperative program that successfully met the after-school needs of children. Following a snack and some recreational games at the local community center, kids were escorted by KEY staff to the library to receive homework assistance. From there, they were then transported back to the community center by parks personnel. A more recent example of interdepartmental cooperation is the Homework Pals program, which, thanks to a partnership between the Monterey Public Library and the parks department, is offered in a recreation center as well as local schools.

As homework centers become more a means of preventing at-risk youth from getting into trouble, librarians are suddenly finding themselves more aligned with law enforcement after-school programs. In Baltimore, Police Athletic League officers run off-site homework centers, equipped with library materials and online public access terminals, in community recreation centers. League members also regularly provide after-school homework assistance in San Diego–area branch libraries. Such programs not only encourage homework success, but foster trusting relationships between the kids and law enforcement officials.

Staff have traditionally depended on the Friends of the Library for financial and in-kind support. In Monroe County, Indiana, and Ojai Valley and Foster City, California, the Friends purchased computer equipment and supplies to help launch their libraries' homework centers. At the Woodrow Wilson Community Library, in Virginia, the Friends not only volunteer as homework assistants, but they also pay for the snacks that are distributed daily as part of the library's after-school program.

Besides Friends groups, many other local organizations also generously support their libraries' homework-assistance programs. A notable example is the YWCA, which donated to the Friendly Stop a $12,000 grant that they themselves had been awarded by the United Way. Although the YWCA's gift was unsolicited, the library gratefully accepted the money to pay for much-needed after-school tutors. In Falls Church, the Virginia Cooperative Extension Service and 4-H Club joined forces with the Woodrow Wilson Community Library to bring homework assistance to a multilingual and culturally diverse student body. For their outstanding efforts, the library and its benefactors were awarded a prestigious community service award in the "partnership" category. An organization called Community of the Light not only donated computers to the Biblioteca Latinoamericana Branch of the San Jose Public Library, but also provides free copy cards for kids to photocopy items in the library. Finally, in Riverside, California, the Easthills Chamber of Commerce has become a valued partner of the library's Cybrary. Not only did the chamber donate materials and labor to help build the facility, but it is now trying to make the program self-sufficient by sponsoring off-hours workshops led by Cybrary staff. For each workshop, the library charges $100 an hour.

Local businesses have also proven to be loyal partners. One of the most successful arrangements has existed for several years in Bloomington, Indiana, where the Monroe County Public Library and the local McDonald's restaurant have paired up to bring math assistance to secondary-school students two nights a week. The joint Math Homework Help program is offered every Monday night at the library and every Wednesday night at McDonald's. In addition, the restaurant heavily advertises both programs twice a year via flyers, which it inserts in all "to-go" orders.

Malls, newspapers, supermarkets, and professional sports teams have all contributed to after-school library programs. In Sacramento, the Kings basketball team purchased a computer for the Martin Luther King Jr. Regional Library homework center. A second basketball team, the Heat, donated a number of incentives to boost participation in the Miami-Dade Public Library System's Heat Homework Partners Program. Inducements included caps, posters, and a grand-prize drawing for a VIP game night featuring preferred seating, dinner for four, a limousine ride to and from the game, and a photo opportunity with the players.

Summary

Acquiring the resources to adequately staff and equip homework centers is an ongoing exercise that continually tests librarians' fund-raising and community-relations skills. Because they can, as nonprofit entities, apply for grants and other funding opportunities not usually made available to government agencies, library foundations are extremely helpful in generating funds for after-school homework programs. Especially lucrative are government grants that target educational and at-risk youth projects. In recent years, libraries have also begun to rely on the generosity of private funders to support what some consider "value-added" services. Financial institutions and local businesses are particularly generous, as are community groups like the Friends of the Library, the YWCA, and chambers of commerce.

7

Collaboration with Schools

Although public libraries and schools share many of the same service goals, bringing the two entities together in a concerted educational effort is often a challenge. Librarians protest mass homework assignments that are impossible to handle using limited resources, while teachers complain that their local public library is not adequately stocked to fulfill their students' needs. The creation of a public library homework center may not resolve these particular issues, but if planned correctly, such a program may present a catalyst for school and library officials to begin working together collaboratively.

The Need for Communication

Librarians and educators agree that one of the main barriers to a child's successful completion of homework is a lack of communication between local schools and the public library. Kids suffer when the library has not received advance notice of homework assignments and when school officials are unaware of library hours and regulations. To strengthen communication, many public librarians hold regularly scheduled information-sharing workshops to introduce K–12 teachers to the library's resources. Educators are also encouraged to make liberal use of "homework alert" forms to notify library staff of upcoming projects. In Poolesville, Maryland, and Bloomington, Indiana, local schools keep the library up-to-date via the fax machine. At the Corvallis–Benton County Public Library in Oregon, not only do teachers alert librarians to class assignments, but they also work with staff to reserve specific items to help students with their projects. These materials are housed near the reference desk for "library use only" during the course of the assignment. In other libraries, staff have found that teachers respond particularly well to incentives. Recently, all teachers who turned in homework alert forms to a branch of the County of Los Angeles Public Library were entered into a drawing for restaurant coupons, map books, and small office supplies.

Communication between the schools and the library improved substantially when it was rewarded.

In Durham, North Carolina, and Baltimore, librarians have compiled lists of "homework tips" to make library visits as worthwhile as possible for both students and teachers. These tips provide helpful homework hints to students and encourage teachers to plan their research assignments carefully. When doing schoolwork in the library, students are advised to

- bring their own supplies, including homework assignments, paper and pencils, money for the photocopier, textbooks, and library cards;
- use electronic as well as print resources;
- keep library hours in mind and not wait until the last minute to complete the assignment;
- ask the librarian for suggestions on how to use library resources; and
- use the library regularly and often.

As for teachers, library staff suggest that they

- assign a choice of reading options, rather than a single title for every student to read;
- avoid "mass assignments" on the same subject;
- notify librarians of homework assignments in advance;
- visit the library to make sure it owns the materials required to complete the assignment;
- accept references from chapters, magazines, and pamphlets, as well as general and specialized encyclopedias;
- provide opportunities for students to do research in the school library;
- give assignments in writing, rather than orally, to eliminate confusion among students;
- stagger major research projects and allow enough time to complete them;
- encourage the use of student-generated illustrations, rather than pictures from magazines or books; and
- remind students that librarians can relay only brief information over the telephone.

For many school officials and librarians, the best communication occurs face-to-face at regularly scheduled events. At the Monroe County Public Library, in Indiana, twenty years of monthly meetings have enriched the relationship between the school librarians and the public library's children's and young adult services staff. As a result, the school corporation and the teachers' union help pay the salary of the lead homework tutor, who provides after-school math assistance to the public library's teen patrons. In Westwood, Massachusetts, school and public library staff meet several times a year to discuss common goals and problems. Teachers are invited to participate in the library's collection development, while public library staff assist with updating school reading lists. The public library also hosts an annual orientation for sixth-graders and their teachers.

Collaborative Efforts

Perhaps the most outstanding example of a combined school–public library homework-assistance effort is the Tall Tree Initiative in Westchester County, New York. Funded by the Reader's Digest Foundation, this multimillion-dollar project strives to create a seamless educational support system for young students. Among the project's many accomplishments is a courier service between the New Rochelle Public Library and the local elementary school; a joint Tall Tree library card that allows kids to borrow from and return materials to either the library or the school site; and a homework hot line where parents and teachers can leave voicemail. Thanks to the Teacher in the Library component of the program, students also receive homework assistance from local teachers who are employed by the public library to work after school. In addition, public librarians regularly visit elementary-school classrooms to teach students how to use software, media, print, and electronic resources.

Another exemplary model of interagency cooperation is the Homework Pals program in Monterey, California. Although the library sponsors and oversees the program, the actual homework assistance is provided off-site as part of the school district's after-school day-care service. Elementary-school children are eligible to participate in the Homework Pals program, which is handled through the various campus day-care centers. The library is responsible for recruiting and training the homework assistants and, in conjunction with the school district, for conducting an annual homework-help-related workshop for parents and the community.

Other public library homework programs have also benefited from collaborative ventures with local schools. In Durham County, North Carolina, the library offered a Homework Hotline or Walk-In service sponsored jointly with the Durham City Schools. The library provided the space and reference materials to carry out the program, while the school system made available textbooks, tutors, and a telephone. In Corvallis, Oregon, the school district permanently "loaned" computer equipment to be used in the library's Homework Alert Centers. Elsewhere, educators have provided special math calculators for young patrons to use at the Allen County Public Library, Indiana, and a collection of K–12 textbooks to the Rolling Meadows Library in Illinois. Kids in Tigard, Oregon, are transported to the library's homework center via school buses, while in Hanson, Massachusetts, administrators installed a paved walkway between the public library and two nearby schools.

Some school districts have also been generous in financially cosponsoring various aspects of the public library's after-school program. In San Mateo County, California, the schools pay the homework-helper's salary at the Foster City Library. Likewise, in Riverside, school officials donated $3,500 to hire Cybrary tutors.

Summary

Although lack of communication has traditionally been a barrier to the successful completion of homework, school and public library officials have begun to work together to bring after-school programs to youth. To improve communication, some librarians regularly meet with or conduct workshops for K–12 teachers; others develop lists of helpful tips to facilitate the homework process. Examples of strong collaborative homework efforts include the Tall Tree Initiative, in New Rochelle, and Homework Pals, in the city of Monterey.

8

Space and Location

Whether the program is offered in an isolated room or is fully integrated into the library's overall floor plan, providing a dedicated area to meet students' after-school needs is essential to the definition of a homework center. Not only does the space itself distinguish a *center* from other types of homework services, such as telephone hot lines or virtual Web sites, but it also gives kids a sense of place where they can make homework a priority. In addition, physical boundaries enable staff to control and constructively focus the energies of the students participating in the program. Because quiet and studious behavior are required to complete one's schoolwork, the library's rules of conduct are often more easily enforceable within the perimeters of the homework center.

Finding the room for even a part-time program may be difficult, however, in an already crowded facility. At one site, for instance, the homework center ended up displacing the library's literacy program, which had previously been located in a secluded part of the stacks. At another, homework assistance competes with after-school story times, which are conducted in the same small area. The noise of children discussing their school assignments may distract other patrons, but remote study rooms may present security risks. Despite these challenges, many librarians have found practical yet creative ways to accommodate the space needed for after-school homework-assistance programs.

Separate Spaces

To control the problem of excitable youth disrupting other patrons after school, several homework programs are held in library meeting rooms located away from the public. The advantages of such an arrangement are apparent. Students can chat among themselves and with their tutors without fear of disturbing other library users, and homework activity can be closely supervised within the confines of the room. Kids may even be allowed to eat and drink while studying in a secluded part of the building. In Northfield, Minnesota, the library's youth advisory board sells healthy snacks as part of the Homework Cafe. Food is also an integral part of the after-school program at the Woodrow Wilson Community Library in Falls Church, Virginia.

Homework-center resources may also be more easily secured and controlled when situated in a self-contained area. Programs like the San Bernadino County Family Technology Learning Center (TLC), which is located in the library's former community room, are less likely to fall victim to vandalism and theft thanks to lockable space. Also, when the room is separate from the rest of the library, the homework area can schedule its own business hours depending on staff availability. Having the center closed during school hours allows administrators to allocate human resources more appropriately.

According to a 1999 study by the American Library Association, 9 percent of all public library homework-assistance programs are held in schools or other community-based organizations. The Friendly Stop, as an outreach effort, was housed in a community center located in the heart of a Latino barrio in Orange, California. The project manager, who spent the morning working at the nearby central library, staffed the homework center in the afternoon once school let out. To support local school curricula, a small collection of bilingual books, magazines, and videos was made available, as was online access to the library's automated catalog. A similar but smaller-scale program is run out of recreation centers in Baltimore, where the Enoch Pratt Free Library and the Police Athletic League have teamed up to provide after-school activities for "at-risk" youth. In New Rochelle, New York, bilingual library assistants provide homework help to children who frequent the local Boys' Club.

Perhaps the single most-successful off-site homework-assistance program is Homework Pals, coordinated by the Monterey Public Library. In this highly innovative program, homework help is offered as part of the after-school day-care service provided by the school district. Elementary-school children who are enrolled in after-school day care may sign up for homework assistance on a daily basis. The local day-care provider then matches up the students with the Pals, who have volunteered to help kids complete that day's homework. All one-on-one assistance is conducted in the school's library or in a vacant classroom. Because the program occurs on school property, library officials are not liable for any security matters that might arise. Instead, the library's main responsibility is to recruit, train, and schedule the volunteers who work at the schools in the afternoon. Homework Pals is effective because homework assistance is delivered to kids right in their own school environment.

Even though staff, students, and the public may prefer separately housed homework-assistance programs, there are distinct disadvantages to such arrangements. Unlike programs that are held in the library's more visible areas, isolated homework centers must, for security reasons, be staffed with on-site personnel every minute they are open. This, in turn, may seriously curtail the number of hours the homework program is offered. In Brooklyn, for instance, math peer tutoring is limited to only one hour a week because of a lack of staff available to supervise the program, which is held in the library's auditorium.

In addition to security-induced scheduling problems, enclosed homework centers may also be limited by the number of hours other organizations need to use that space. The Homework Cafe, for example, is open only one afternoon a week because the Northfield

Public Library's meeting room is in high demand by other agencies. In Orange, the homework center was almost dissolved when the school district, which owned the building in which the Friendly Stop was located, decided it had other more lucrative uses for that space. A homework program that consistently occupies valuable space requires an enormous commitment on the part of the library and cosponsoring agency, especially if that space could otherwise be used to generate revenue through room rental or other fees.

A corollary disadvantage to off-site or separately located homework centers is the possible lack of a "library context" for homework activities. If one of the purposes of the program is to instill good library habits, a homework center housed in a community room, recreation center, or school may not necessarily achieve that goal. Instead, children will identify more with typically "nonlibrary" space than with book collections, online catalogs, and reference librarians. Also, certain library-related services may have to be replicated if the homework center is too far removed from the rest of the library. For instance, staff of the remote Family TLC soon discovered a need for their own small book collection and photocopy machine.

Nonpublic spaces may also intimidate certain students. Teenage women may feel threatened by a room filled with males. Other students may avoid the homework center altogether if they have to share space with the "wrong crowd" or even younger or older kids. Enclosed areas may even prompt in and out "cruising" by youngsters waiting for their friends to arrive.

Integrated Floor Plans

In facilities without meeting rooms or secluded spaces, homework assistance is generally conducted on the library floor. In fact, in some libraries, like New Rochelle, Oakland's César E. Chavéz Branch, and Allen County, the entire children's or young adult section is converted into a homework center after school. In smaller outlets, such as the Castroville Library, Seattle Public Library's High Point Branch, and Santa Cruz City-County Library's Garfield Park Branch, the whole building becomes a hub of after-school activity, with homework as the top priority for both staff and students.

Although open-area homework centers may present noise and other control problems, for the most part librarians report positive results from such programs. Comfortably surrounded by books and computers, kids begin to think of the library as a "place of their own" and may even return during nonschool days. Homework areas need not be large, but they should always be clearly defined so that appropriate behaviors can be enforced while participating in the program. At the County of Los Angeles Public Library, staff recommend that homework centers be visible to enhance security. Corner spaces are preferred because they tend to identify the area as something unique and special. The look and location of the homework center should also reflect the age group being targeted. Teenagers, for example, may refuse to study in the children's room, while elementary-school kids may feel out of place in the young adult area.

One of the most effective uses of after-school library space is the Student Express at the Enoch Pratt Free Library. Located on a second-floor mezzanine of the central library, the Student Express was created specifically to meet the curricular needs of adolescents. The area is staffed by a young adult services librarian who not only answers reference questions, but also oversees activity at the center's many tables. Although the Student Express remains open during all library business hours, it is, of course, busiest after school, when kids avail themselves of the homework center's extensive collection of print and electronic resources.

Equally impressive is the Sony Pictures Homework Center in Culver City, California. Bounded by low shelves, the area is clearly visible from the reference and circulation desks yet isolated enough to give kids a sense of privacy. At the heart of the center is a circular bank of computers donated by Sony Studios. Also available are open cabinets where student backpacks can be stored. What clearly distinguishes this area from the rest of the library is a monolithic arch created by a movie set designer. Once they pass through the brightly colored archway, kids know they must focus on their homework; otherwise, they will be asked to leave. The space is so popular that even during unsupervised periods, young library patrons can be found there quietly working on their school assignments.

Less distinctive but just as effective is the homework area at the East Palo Alto Library. Located near the library's entrance within clear view of staff and patrons, a "homework only" zone is created every weekday afternoon by using large orange road "cones" to mark the boundaries of the program. A clublike atmosphere is promoted through an application process that admits only those students who have demonstrated a commitment to schoolwork. To use one of the handful of tables within the prestigious coned-off area, kids must exhibit appropriate studious behavior or they will be asked to sit in another part of the library.

Signage

Just as important as a well-situated homework center are appealing signage and other clever methods of attracting kids to the library. Part of the allure of Culver City's homework program is no doubt the Sony Pictures name emblazoned above the entryway. At Enoch Pratt, the Student Express is easily located thanks to a flashy neon sign. A distinctive globe-shaped poster also indicates Enoch Pratt's Whole New World workstations, which provide curriculum support via the Internet.

At the Colonial Heights Branch in Sacramento, eye-catching graphics not only point the way to the library's secluded homework area, but also credit the Naygrow Family Foundation with sponsoring the program. In addition, a distinctive logo is used to post the homework-center's hours on the library's front door.

Colors may also effectively identify homework-help areas. At the Mason/Ramsdell Library in Massachusetts, bright footprints appear on the floor leading kids and their parents to the reference room in which the homework center is located. In Hennepin County, beautiful pastels are used to attract children to the library's KidLinks program. All signs and publicity are bathed in mauve, gold, and blue, as are the KidLinks furnishings.

Summary

Providing a dedicated space to meet students' after-school needs is essential, because kids need a place where they can make homework a priority. Physical boundaries also enable staff to control and constructively focus the energies of the students participating in the program. Although finding adequate space may be difficult in already crowded facilities, many librarians have found practical yet creative ways to accommodate after-school homework-assistance programs. In particular, library meeting rooms and even nonlibrary sites are effective locations for homework centers. Such spaces need constant supervision, however, and may compete with other agencies for use. In addition, off-site programs tend to lack a library context. Although open-area homework centers present noise and other control problems, librarians have reported positive results from such arrangements. Notable examples of in-library homework centers are found in Baltimore, Culver City, and East Palo Alto. Just as important as a well-situated homework center are appealing signage and eye-catching colors.

9

Service Hours

According to the American Library Association, after-school homework help is the most consistently scheduled program in public libraries that provide such a service once a week or more. Indeed, of the libraries surveyed for this 1999 study, more than 80 percent offer formal homework assistance three to seven days a week. Yet, like everything else related to homework centers, no two sets of schedules are alike.

Assessing Community Need

Unfortunately, many homework-assistance hours seem more driven by library resources than by community need. The fewer staff available to oversee the program, the less hours the homework center is open. In Brooklyn, math peer tutoring is offered only one hour a week because of a lack of staff. Likewise, in Bloomington, Indiana, math help is available at the library on Monday nights only, because of limited resources. Kids may be interested in receiving homework assistance all week long, but without adequate funding, the service is often restricted to the resources at hand.

At the County of Los Angeles Public Library, administrators recommend that staff consider the needs of the community first when designing the homework center's schedule. At what time do schools let out? When do kids have access to the library? On what days do school holidays usually fall? Once these questions are answered, then a viable itinerary can be developed and appropriate staff hired. Above all else, schedules should reflect community need. As a prime example, the homework helper at one branch of the San Jose Public Library makes appointments with kids based on the individual student's availability.

Scheduling Factors

Although it may seem obvious that *after-school* programs should occur between the hours of 3:00 and 6:00 P.M., several factors must be considered when scheduling homework help. If the main purpose of the homework center is to manage a chronic unattended-children situation, then the program should be offered directly after school when parents and other caregivers are working. To preclude a free after-school day-care scenario, staff may decide to stagger the days in which the service is provided. For instance, at a now-defunct program in San Leandro, California, students were allowed to sign up for homework assistance on Monday and Wednesday or Tuesday and Thursday, but not all four days. On the alternate days, kids were encouraged to visit day-care facilities elsewhere so the library would not become the only after-school option for local unattended children.

When planning homework programs for older kids, librarians must consider that today's youth are extremely busy. With part-time jobs, mandatory community service, and sports activities, homework may play a minor role in a high-school student's daily routine. At the Minneapolis Public Library, homework assistance is offered on Saturdays and until 7:00 P.M. two nights a week to meet the curricular needs of those kids tasked with baby-sitting their younger siblings after school. In Fort Wayne, Indiana, homework help is scheduled even later, from 6:30 to 8:30 P.M., to allow active students time to eat dinner before coming to the library.

Staff must also consider that not all youngsters have ready access to transportation. If the homework center is located in a remote or notoriously dangerous part of town, then services must be scheduled early enough to allow kids to walk home safely during daylight. At the Friendly Stop, children always left before dark; therefore, business hours were changed according to the season to account for earlier and later sunsets.

Although some librarians find Saturday to be their busiest homework-help day, others have canceled weekend programs because of a lack of interest. Many schools apparently do not assign homework over the weekend, when kids are otherwise occupied. Friday may also be a slow homework day for some libraries. At the Sacramento Public Library, staff noted a 100 percent increase in homework-center attendance when Friday was dropped from the schedule and Monday added. To attract kids to the library in Houston, Friday has become "game day," when educational activities are offered rather than the usual homework assistance.

Summer and Holidays

Even if school is not offered during the summer, some libraries operate their homework programs year-round. During June and July, the homework center may be transformed into the library's summer reading club or the site of other noncurricular educational activities. At the Sacramento Public Library, staff of the Cool Summer Homework Center offer contests and weekly programs to encourage visits to the library. Hours are also changed to reflect earlier summer-school release times. In San Bernardino County, the Family Technology Learning Center (TLC) opens at noon during the summer to attract kids not in school.

Winter can wreak havoc on homework-assistance schedules, especially in regions where schools are regularly closed for "snow days." In Fairfax County, Virginia, and Tigard, Oregon, homework help is offered only on days when school is in session. For most other libraries, homework centers are closed during holidays and over the two-week Christmas vacation. One librarian, in fact, finds fall and winter holidays so disruptive that she recommends starting the homework program's annual cycle well before November so kids can get into the habit of coming to the library every day after school.

Summary

Although it may seem obvious that after-school programs occur between the hours of 3:00 and 6:00 P.M., several factors should be considered when scheduling homework help. Among these factors are school schedules, the age of the students being served, whether the kids have ready access to transportation, and which days homework is assigned. Above all else, staff should consider the needs of the community first when designing the homework-center's schedule.

10 | *Programming and Corollary Services*

Besides assistance with schoolwork, many public libraries offer programming and other corollary services as part of their homework-center operations. Although they may be offered primarily as part of an overall plan to keep kids constructively occupied during critical after-school hours, these activities are nonetheless motivated by the library's sincere desire to support the learning needs of its younger constituents.

Educational Activities

In most after-school homework programs designed specifically for children, educational "contingency" activities are made available for those students who finish their homework quickly. These may include board games, work sheets, and even educational software and are often used as incentives to motivate children to complete their schoolwork. At the Woodrow Wilson Community Library, in Falls Church, Virginia, the first hour of the after-school program is dedicated to homework help, with educational games and activities following as the children finish their class assignments. In Queens Borough, homework-center staff lead kids in story times and crafts once their schoolwork is completed.

At one Sacramento Public Library branch, staff posts several "questions of the week" on a bulletin board in the homework-center area. Brainteasers such as "Make up as many words as you can from the word *homework*" and "Which means the same as 'give advice'— council or counsel?" test students on vocabulary, spelling skills, and math. The winners are rewarded with small prizes, and their names are posted on the bulletin board. Participants in Sacramento's homework program also contribute to the library's *Homework Center Gazette*, which features students' writing samples and science-fair projects. Perfect attendance at the homework center is also noted, as are student birthdays.

In Oakland, a survey discovered that participants in the library's PASS! (Partners for Achieving School Success) program typically help each other or library staff after completing their homework. They also play educational games, write in journals, or do some other creative-writing activity. Seventy-two percent of the students surveyed also indicated that they use after-school time for pleasure reading.

Enrichment Programming

In addition to strictly educational activities, many libraries also offer life-enriching programs that teach new skills, expose kids to new ideas, and help them develop their decision-making abilities. At the Friendly Stop, in Orange, California, staff regularly invited speakers to discuss such diverse topics as birth control, AIDS, racism, drugs, job searching, filmmaking, airbrush design, and how to make salsa. Author Helen Viramontes read from her works to a roomful of teens while relating her experiences as a young Latina in East Los Angeles. In Castroville, California, homework-center staff and the migrant-education counselor of a nearby high school invite a college representative to the library every year to explain the financial-aid process and help students fill out the necessary forms.

At the Houston Public Library, programming is an integral part of the ASPIRE (After School Programs Inspire Reading Enrichment) program. In one month alone, the library offered a career presentation on dentistry, a talk on "The History of Buffalo Soldiers and the West," a "Black History Bowl" competition, and a program by the Zietor African Ensemble. During the summer, regular activities include a creative-writing camp, a Texas-history treasure hunt, *Jeopardy!* game competitions, a music festival, T-shirt craft days, martial arts demonstrations, cheerleading camp, and an ASPIRE talent show.

Special events may also be used as incentives for kids to consistently participate in the homework program. At the East Palo Alto Branch, in San Mateo County, California, students earn points for regularly attending the library's after-school homework center. Once the kids earn the requisite number of points, they are invited on a field trip coordinated by the lead homework tutor. Two of the more memorable field trips included tickets to an Alvin Ailey dance concert and an all-day outing at Stanford University.

In some libraries, after-school programs are presented primarily to entertain and demonstrate just how fun learning can be. The Monterey Public Library has, as part of its Homework Pals program, sponsored events featuring a creative math wiz and "The Bubble Man," a performer who manipulates bubbles. At the Toledo–Lucas County Public Library, special monthly programs, such as a petting zoo, professional storytellers, magicians, and puppeteers, are offered to provide local children an opportunity to experience things they might otherwise miss.

Summary

In addition to providing assistance with schoolwork, many public libraries offer programming and other corollary services as part of their homework-center operations. These activities may include access to educational games and extracurricular events, such as author readings, lectures, competitions, talent shows, and field trips. Regardless of the format, these special activities are always designed with the learning needs of the library's young patrons in mind.

11

Collection Development

In a community that offers several after-school homework-assistance options, the collection is often what distinguishes the public library's homework center from all the rest. Indeed, because librarians tend to consider books and electronic resources the basis of good homework assistance, the collection is one of the defining elements of the library's after-school program. Providing materials to support students' needs is, after all, what libraries have always done best.

Collection Development Considerations

Depending on the library, the homework-assistance collection may consist of a small bookshelf or cart filled with a limited number of ready-reference titles or may encompass the entire youth-services section. At the Allen County Public Library, in Indiana, for example, titles that support the local curriculum are fully integrated into the overall young adult collection. Size and placement of the homework-center collection should reflect not only patron needs and space availability, but also the extent to which the collection duplicates or complements nearby school libraries. Before the collection is created, staff should determine whether students need supplemental materials to complete their homework or if assignments are based strictly on reading the textbook. Also, is a special reference collection necessary to meet the needs of multiple students or is the circulating collection adequate? Finally, what types of media are kids required to use when researching class assignments?

When establishing a homework-assistance collection, librarians may pull items from other parts of the library to expedite the development process. For instance, at Enoch Pratt, in Maryland, materials on science-fair projects, literary criticism, career guidance, and popular social science topics were borrowed from other parts of the library to create the

Student Express collection. Likewise in Culver City, books on recurring school themes were relocated to the homework center to facilitate the research process. Among the most prevalent subjects and types of materials collected by homework-center staff are

- standard encyclopedias;
- dictionaries;
- almanacs;
- thesauri;
- science encyclopedias;
- atlases;
- biographies and biographical dictionaries;
- mathematics books;
- science experiments;
- general and local history, such as books on Southwestern missions;
- geography and culture;
- Native American tribes;
- books on how to write reports and essays;
- career guidance;
- mythology;
- endangered species;
- U.S. presidents;
- social science topics; and
- literary criticism.

If the library has the space, pamphlets and magazines are also valuable homework-help tools. In addition, homework centers may carry materials in international languages, based on local demographics. Staff should be particularly sensitive to the community's needs, however, when selecting non-English-language materials. At the Friendly Stop, a great deal of expense and effort went into developing a Spanish-language collection, only to discover later that neighborhood parents preferred their children using English-language sources when doing homework. In Oakland, on the other hand, having access to materials in both Spanish and English gives bilingual students twice the resource options when researching especially popular topics.

Staff may also want to consider making textbooks available through the homework center. Although public librarians have traditionally eschewed purchasing school texts, today the value of providing such a resource is apparent. Because many students either forget or are not allowed to bring their textbooks home, librarians and homework assistants are often handicapped in trying to help kids with their assignments. In Rolling Meadows, Illinois, this problem became so severe that the youth-services staff and the school district joined forces to make available a set of K–12 textbooks at the public library. An average of three students used the books nightly, with greater use reported on the weekend. Furthermore, by using the texts themselves, staff gained a better understanding of the school curriculum and could locate supplemental materials more easily. Libraries in Brooklyn, Oakland, San Bernardino County, Allen County, and Minneapolis all supply copies of school textbooks whenever possible. In New Rochelle, this service was discontinued because of an ever-changing curriculum.

Electronic Resources

Besides print resources, many public libraries also provide a variety of electronic homework-assistance tools. These may be offered as networked CD-ROM products or preselected Internet sites. At the Houston Public Library, very specific collection development statements guide ASPIRE (After School Programs Inspire Reading Enrichment) staff in selecting all print and nonprint sources. Only educational software that provide an entertaining learning experience are collected in the areas of science, math, language arts, and social studies. Web sites, moreover, are evaluated according to their reference value, ease of use, source and/or authority, age appropriateness, and currency. The following are among the many sites linked to the ASPIRE home page:

Electric Library	http://www.elibrary.com/s/edumark/
School Work!	http://www.schoolwork.org/
Teen Hoopla	http://www.ala.org/teenhoopla/homework.html
Study Web	http://www.studyweb.com
Encyclopedia.com	http://www.encyclopedia.com/
Information Please	http://www.infoplease.com
My Virtual Reference Desk	http://www.refdesk.com
Afro-American Almanac	http://www.toptags.com/aama/
Corbis	http://www.corbis.com
Cultural Maps	http://xroads.virginia.edu/~MAP/map_hp.html

One of the most popular services offered by the Cybrary is in-library access to dozens of educational CD-ROMs. The cover of the product's outer package is laminated and filed in a notebook for easy patron access. The following are among the more than one hundred titles made available at the Cybrary:

- Animals in Danger
- Elroy Goes Bugzerk
- Encyclopedia of Nature
- Where in the World Is Carmen Sandiego?
- The Hispanic-American Experience
- Amazon Trail II
- Castle Explorer
- The Development of Technology
- How Would You Survive?
- Women in America
- Time Almanac of the 20th Century
- Carmen Sandiego, Math Detective
- Math Blaster

- Carmen Sandiego, Word Detective
- How to Read a Book and Live to Tell about It
- Reading Blaster
- 3-D Explorer USA
- American Heritage Talking Dictionary
- Encyclopedia Encarta
- Student Reference Library
- The Visual Dictionary
- Bill Nye, the Science Bus
- Body Works
- Planetary Taxi
- The Way Things Work
- Typing Teacher

Summary

Because it often distinguishes the public library's homework center from all the rest, the collection is one of the defining elements of the library's after-school program. When developing the homework-support collection, staff should consider patron needs, space availability, and the extent to which the collection duplicates and/or complements nearby school libraries. Homework-assistance collections may include reference and nonfiction print titles, non-English-language materials, textbooks, and a variety of electronic resources.

12

Supplies and Equipment

W hether they are purchased by outside sources, such as Friends of the Library groups, or provided for as part of the library's general budget, most homework programs require a certain amount of supplies and equipment to be effective. Provisions may include everything from simple school supplies to elaborate computer workstations, depending on community needs and the resources available. Supplying forgetful or low-income students with even the most basic items, like pencils and paper, may go a long way toward helping them complete their homework.

Standard Homework Supplies

Although librarians have always kept scratch paper and extra pencils on hand for young patrons to use after school, homework-center staff have developed extensive lists of supplies required to facilitate the homework process. Among the most common items stocked by the various homework centers are

- writing implements, such as pencils, pens, markers, and crayons;
- erasers;
- paper of various kinds, such as loose-leaf paper, typing paper, index cards, graph paper, construction paper, Post-it Notes, and wide-lined paper for younger students;
- math supplies, such as flash cards, rulers, compasses, protractors, and calculators;
- office supplies, such as scissors, staplers, staple remover, three-hole punch, whiteout, paper clips, tape, and glue sticks; and
- file folders.

One library even supplies earplugs for students who need complete quiet. Libraries also provide computer disks, either gratis or for a small fee. At the San Bernadino County Family Technology Learning Center (TLC), a disk is given to each person who registers to use the equipment. The disks are then kept on file at the Family TLC to minimize the spread of computer viruses.

In her book on organizing after-school programs for at-risk youth, Tommie Morton-Young recommends that artifacts, models, and objects be made available as learning resources. In Oakland, a clock is included as part of all PASS! supply kits. At the Toledo–Lucas County Public Library, in Ohio, the homework center carries a world globe. Kids have access to an abacus in New Rochelle.

To organize and control the flow of items, homework supplies are often kept secured in large plastic boxes that are brought out after school. At the Monterey Public Library, each Homework Pals site has its own stock of supplies. New Rochelle tutors are presented with a box filled with paper, pencils, flash cards, forms, and so forth. In Oakland, PASS! supplies are housed on a book truck that is wheeled into the homework area every afternoon. Kids and tutors help themselves as appropriate. Likewise, at one branch of the San Jose Public Library, supplies are kept in a plastic cabinet short enough for even the youngest student to access.

Furnishings

Because few libraries can afford to dedicate permanent space to their homework centers, most programs do not require special furnishings. Still, there are ways to make the homework area a unique place, even with very limited resources. At the Community Learning Center of South San Francisco Public Library, the furniture in the children's section is labeled as the "math table" or "reading table," so kids know exactly where to go to receive homework help in those subjects.

One of the simplest ways of distinguishing homework-center space is by mounting an eye-catching bulletin board where regulations and relevant announcements can be posted. At the Seaside Branch of the Monterey Free County Libraries, the homework-program's "vision" statement appears alongside articles on how to successfully complete class assignments. In Oakland, the names of PASS! "students of the week" are displayed on the children's room bulletin board. A contest featuring "homework questions of the week" is posted in Sacramento.

Another relatively inexpensive but useful piece of equipment is a whiteboard, where group homework assignments can be tackled by students and their tutors. In Bloomington, Indiana, the whiteboard is particularly helpful in diagramming mathematics problems as part of the library's math-assistance program.

Computer Equipment

Although access to computer equipment is not mandatory for an effective after-school program, computers are becoming more essential to the homework process. Students are often required to use the Internet as a resource and may even receive higher grades for turning in word-processed papers. Yet not all kids have computers at home. In fact, according to the U.S. Department of Commerce, libraries are the number-one point of access to the Internet for low-income and single-parent families. Indeed, in a survey of Santa Cruz teenagers, library officials discovered that everyone felt a need for more and better technology. In addition to the Internet, 83 percent of the youth interviewed requested access to CD-ROM products, while 67 percent expressed a desire for word-processing equipment.

To meet the needs of their technologically underprivileged patrons, several libraries make computer access the central focus of their homework programs. Of particular note are the Los Angeles Public Library, Hennepin County's KidLinks program, Enoch Pratt's Whole New World, San Bernardino County's Family TLC, and Riverside Public Library's Cybrary. In-library computer training is often included as part of the homework-assistance program, and in many cases, students are allowed to print up to ten computer-generated pages for free. In Los Angeles, older computers are recycled as stand-alone word processors for kids to use in the central library's teen center. At the Castroville Library, young patrons are taught how to repair donated computers, which they are then allowed to take home.

Fortunately, outside agencies seem most amenable to funding library projects that promote computer access. The use of the equipment is readily apparent, as is a belief that computer-literate students will one day make the country more economically competitive. Friends groups and even school districts have been instrumental in providing computers to their local libraries. On a larger scale, the Gates Foundation has generously equipped several public library homework centers with Microsoft products. The Reader's Digest Foundation, through its Tall Tree Initiative, has also supplied computers to New York–area libraries.

Despite the generosity of these and other benefactors, staff still find themselves limiting access to the library's computers because of a demand that far exceeds the resources available. At both the Enoch Pratt Free Library and the Cybrary, youngsters must pass an in-library training course before being allowed to use the Internet or the library's other electronic resources. At other sites, students are required to sign up for equipment use, with access limited to twenty minutes to an hour, depending on the library. Moreover, computers located within the study area are generally designated as "homework use only" during after-school hours. Although some libraries may allow up to two people to use a single computer, others restrict usage to one person per machine to control noise levels. Headphones are also made available to help alleviate the sounds generated by various software.

Because the library's homework center may be equipped with some of the most advanced technology in the community, securing the computers against vandalism and theft can be a challenge. At one library, the homework-center's computers remain locked until the students arrive and then are closely supervised by the site coordinator. At another, software hacking became so prevalent that staff resorted to checking out keyboards for in-library use. A programmed security system was also installed to protect the library's Windows software.

Summary

Homework-center provisions include everything from simple school supplies to sophisticated computer workstations. Although most programs do not require special furnishings, there are ways to make the homework space unique. Bulletin boards and whiteboards are especially useful for posting homework-center rules and announcements and for helping solve group assignments. Although access to computer equipment is not mandatory for an effective after-school program, computers are becoming more essential to the homework process. In fact, staff must often limit access to the library's computers because of a demand that far exceeds the resources available.

13

Security and Liability

Although most public libraries strive to provide a safe learning environment after school, few librarians consider their programs completely risk free. Libraries are, after all, public venues and therefore vulnerable to outside dangers. Still, youngsters must feel safe in the library so they will be encouraged to return. Students and their parents must also be made to fully understand the intent of the library's homework program. Are kids guaranteed personalized help with their schoolwork or is the homework center just a place to study and consult library resources? To avoid problems with liability and false expectations, administrators must carefully define the limitations as well as the purpose of the library's homework program.

Program Security

When the library first introduced the homework-help program in Montclair, New Jersey, one young student expressed apprehension about working with adult strangers. Although no library can assure a completely secure after-school environment, many do try to minimize threats through diligent hiring practices and thoughtful placement of the homework center. Most libraries require a security check or fingerprinting when hiring homework-center staff. Even volunteers are required to complete application forms that request information about past criminal records. In one California library, the homework-program coordinator regularly checks volunteers' names against lists of convicted child abusers, made available through "Megan's Law." At the County of Los Angeles Public Library, only those folks referred by local schools or colleges are hired as homework helpers.

Once hired, most homework staff, whether paid or voluntary, are trained how to appropriately deal with after-school patrons. Mentoring of young students may be encouraged but is never allowed outside the library's walls. Homework staff are also forbidden from giving students a ride home. To distinguish homework helpers from other adults in the library, name badges are often required. In Multnomah County, Oregon, homework assistants wear bright green aprons.

Programs offered in the open as part of the library's regular service obviously present less security risk. Separate homework areas may be designated but should always be visible enough to easily monitor activities. In Foster City, the after-school homework program is situated in a conference room located off the library's lobby. During homework hours, the room's door remains open, as do the drapes of a floor-to-ceiling window overlooking the parking lot. Not only is this a good way to attract students, but safety is ensured because the space is clearly visible to all passersby.

For security reasons, some programs may not allow adults inside the homework center. Others, on the other hand, require that a parent be present in the library while the child is receiving homework help. This not only helps to mitigate liability risks, but also precludes the parent from using the homework center as a drop-off day-care service. The child is also much safer leaving the building with the parent than waiting alone for a ride after the library closes.

Clarifying Expectations

Staff must be careful to promote realistic outcomes when touting the benefits of the library's homework program. To minimize false expectations, libraries may opt to provide merely a "monitored studying environment" rather than a program that guarantees formal homework assistance. Librarians may also choose to avoid all promises of tutorial help, because in many states such service often denotes licensed educational support. Instead of "tutors," the library's homework-assistance providers may be called "helpers," "mentors," "coaches," "pals," or "learning partners."

In her book on how to operate a community-based educational service, Tommie Morton-Young recommends avoiding misunderstandings by clearly stating in writing what the after-school program can and cannot do. Certainly homework-center staff can commit to offering students a variety of services, including a safe and enriching after-school environment, opportunities to use various learning materials, guidance from peers or adult mentors or both, and limited homework assistance. But students and their parents must also be made to understand the homework-center's limitations. Library staff should never guarantee an improvement in a student's grades, nor should staff be expected to act as baby-sitters. In Santa Ana, a flyer addressed to parents and guardians succinctly outlines both the adult's and the child's obligations in making the homework program succeed. Parents are admonished to wait for their children outside the center, while children are warned that they will be asked to leave if they do not follow the library's rules of conduct. Both parties are also reminded that the center's computers are primarily for use by students working on school-related projects and that staff are not responsible for completing a child's homework.

Many libraries require signed registration forms to ensure that all participants fully understand the homework-program's parameters (*see* appendix I for sample registration forms). At the San Bernadino County Family Technology Learning Center, a formal user agreement outlines regulations regarding appropriate computer use and homework-lab restrictions. In Sacramento, parental permission is required before students are allowed to participate in the library's homework activities. By signing the document, parents acknowledge that the library is not a day-care center and that the child is responsible for certain well-mannered behaviors. Students must also sign the form, agreeing to follow the library's rules. To reflect the community's demographics, registration forms are available in Russian as well as Spanish and English.

Summary

Although no public library is completely safe, dangers can be minimized through diligent hiring practices and thoughtful placement of the homework center. Because no program is risk free, administrators need to state very clearly the purpose of the library's homework center. In addition, staff must be careful to promote realistic outcomes when touting the benefits of the program, including a statement of what the service does and does not provide.

14 | Media and Public Relations

Good publicity is imperative if the homework program is to attract potential users. In his book on developing public library services for youth at risk, Stan Weisner recommends creating an overall public relations plan to publicize the library's program. Steps in this plan include

- designing an overall theme that appeals to the public and media alike,
- developing and publicizing newsworthy special events and programs,
- preparing user-friendly publicity materials, and
- using existing communications channels whenever available.

Regardless of the method, publicity campaigns must target students as well as parents, teachers, volunteers, funding agencies, and governing bodies—for without the support of all these groups, the library's homework program will not succeed.

Developing a Theme

A theme is necessary to capture the uniqueness of the homework center. This theme may incorporate a slogan and various visual clues, such as a logo or specific color palette. In Riverside, California, the Cybrary's logo combines images of both a book and a computer, symbolizing the program's emphasis on print as well as electronic resources. In Orange, California, a welcoming hand adorned all Friendly Stop publicity. At the Enoch Pratt Free Library, in Baltimore, the neon sign directing teens to the Student Express has become that service's logo and an inspiration for brightly colored brochures. Pastels not only distinguish KidLinks publications, but also enliven after-school furnishings at the Hennepin County Library, in Minnesota. The homework area is immediately recognizable thanks to its distinctive thematic color scheme.

Special Events

One of the most newsworthy events the library can stage is a "grand opening," where the community is invited to see firsthand what exactly the homework center looks like and does. Not only does such an event celebrate the start of a worthwhile new library service, but it may also be used as a public forum for thanking funders and important political allies. At the Los Angeles Public Library, a dedication ceremony marks the opening of every new homework center. Invited onto the dais alongside library officials are the mayor (or his representative), the local city council member, a member of the library foundation's board, and all donors. Local politicians get to witness how much their constituents value the library, while the donors are praised for making the homework program possible. When the Enoch Pratt Free Library initiated its Whole New World after-school effort, a representative from the Maryland governor's office attended the kickoff ceremony. Vice President Al Gore Jr. also sent his regards.

Large events may also be used to advertise ongoing services, especially to those community members not accessible through traditional English-language media. To bring attention to the barrio-based Friendly Stop, staff held a daylong Día de la Familia/Day of the Family festival on the facility's front lawn. More than four hundred local residents enjoyed mariachis, a traditional Mexican fashion show, ballet *folklorico*, a juggler, a rapper, an art exhibit, and an *ofrenda*, a memorial altar, honoring Latin American artist Frida Kahlo. Likewise, in Long Beach, California, a Cambodian dance program was hosted to publicize the library's After-School Study Center. Although a festival and a dance program may not seem related to the goals of a homework center, both events went far toward strengthening relations with local residents and drew many newcomers into the library.

User-Friendly Publicity

Distributing library-generated flyers is one of the most effective and least expensive ways of advertising homework programs. Indeed, in this way a majority of students learned of the Brooklyn Public Library's math peer-tutoring service. Well-designed flyers include information about the purpose of the program, location, hours of service, telephone number, and intended audience (for examples, *see* appendix J). Because they are portable, flyers can be easily mailed to schools, newspapers, and local organizations. At the Monterey County Free Libraries, homework-center announcements are sent home with class report cards; in San Jose, flyers are distributed through local housing projects. Twice a year the McDonald's restaurant in Bloomington, Indiana, inserts ads for the library's math-assistance program in all carryout food orders.

Eye-catching trinkets emblazoned with the homework-center's name, logo, and telephone number are yet another clever way of attracting potential patrons. Decorated pencils and pens have always worked well as program incentives. But today's kids are much more sophisticated. At the Friendly Stop, T-shirts were awarded to students who regularly used the facility. Globe-shaped key chains advertise Enoch Pratt's Whole New World program.

Yo-yos remind Minneapolis kids to use the library after school. And in Houston, ASPIRE (After School Programs Inspire Reading Enrichment) shoelaces are all the rage.

Web pages, of course, are becoming a more prominent means of publicizing programs. An outstanding example of a homework-center Web site is that of Houston Public Library's ASPIRE program, located at <http://www.hpl.lib.tx.us/youth/aspire/>. This colorful site not only features pictures of kid participants, but also includes a description of the ASPIRE program, service hours, and a statement of intended audience (i.e., fifth- through ninth-graders). "My Rules for Online Safety" is also posted and must be read before a user can proceed to the next screen. Linked to the ASPIRE Web page are a calendar of program events, online homework-help sites, ASPIRE branch locations, online educational-game sites, recruitment information for potential volunteer tutors, and an ASPIRE message board. Users who click on "What is ASPIRE?" are led to a description of a "typical day" in the program; a list of "key program components," including activities, staffing, and available equipment; a brief historical background; future plans; and assessment methods.

Media and Schools

Whenever possible, librarians should make use of existing communications channels to reach their various constituents. Chamber of commerce newsletters, Friends of the Library publications, church circulars, PTA bulletins, and homeowner-association newsletters are all good outlets for free publicity. Television, radio, and newspapers are also important sources for broad-based media coverage. Homework-center openings make interesting news stories, as do after-school programs that serve certain at-risk populations. A retired engineer once volunteered his services to the Friendly Stop after reading an expository piece about the program in the *Los Angeles Times*. When the Oakland Public Library opened its first after-school tutoring center, staff held a press conference featuring the California State Librarian and a well-known young adult author. The homework program in Falls Church, Virginia, has attracted reporters from the *Washington Post*, as well as NBC television, thanks to the unique multicultural mix of the library's after-school users.

Effective public relations may also be accomplished by working with local schools. In Sacramento, homework-center staff make a point of being part of Back to School Night at the beginning of every academic year. At the Seaside Library, in Monterey County, staff hold an annual open house for school principals and district superintendents. Young adult librarians attend faculty meetings to promote the Allen County Public Library's homework-assistance efforts. In Fort Wayne, Indiana, staff work with school counselors to refer students to the library's homework-help program. Elsewhere, a library and school district cosponsored a student competition to design the homework-program logo, and in one California city, a link was established to the homework center from the local high-school's Web page.

Summary

A publicity plan is important to attract users to the homework center. Such a plan may include steps to design a theme or logo that indicates the uniqueness of the homework program; the development of newsworthy special events and programs; preparation of user-friendly publicity materials; and effective use of existing communications channels, including community publications, mass media, and school contacts.

15

Methods of Assessing Effectiveness

As Rosellen Brewer wisely observed regarding her library's homework center, if after-school programs are to continue to be funded, then librarians must find a way to evaluate the effectiveness of such service. Staff who work with students on a daily basis may intuitively understand the value of formal homework assistance, but funders need "hard data" to justify financial support. Although some libraries rely strictly on simple head counts and anecdotal evidence to measure the success of their homework programs, others have developed more sophisticated means of assessment. These methods may include surveys, homework "fill rates," and focus-group interviews.

Assessment Factors

According to former Bay Area Youth at Risk Project director and author Stan Weisner, there are three reasons for evaluating an after-school library program:

1. to determine whether the program is working,
2. to identify the need for improvement or change, and
3. to document success in order to build support for continued funding.

The first step in measuring the effectiveness of a homework center is to clearly state a set of goals and objectives—that is, proposed outcomes—for the program. Satisfactory attainment of these outcomes is then measured through the assessment process. Although it may be difficult to isolate measures directly attributable to the effectiveness of after-school library service, the program evaluator should be able to assess whether the homework center is

- accomplishing its stated goals and objectives,
- reaching its target population, and
- having an impact on the lives of the students being served.

The evaluator should also be able to decipher the quantity and quality of the homework assistance offered as part of the program.

Quantitative Assessment Methods

One of the most common ways of measuring the homework-center's success is through a daily usage count. Whether they are collected through a sign-in sheet or as an anonymous tally, the importance of these figures can be fully realized only when placed within a larger context. In her book on measuring the output of young adult library services, Virginia A. Walter recommends calculating the percentage of homework-center visits by the entire target population (e.g., all teenagers in the community). By dividing the number of homework-center visits by the total number of teens, for example, the evaluator can judge how popular the program is among that group and whether the target population is being served. Walter cautions, however, that unless the homework program is phenomenally popular, visits per target group member will probably equal less than 1 percent if attendance is measured against an entire community.

Another important statistic related to homework-center visits is the comparison between total daily attendance and repeat customers. According to Walter, 20 percent of homework-center participants typically account for 80 percent of the program's use. A high percentage of repeat visitors may indicate satisfaction with the program and, therefore, may be considered a measure of success. Librarians should be careful in interpreting these figures, however, especially in unattended-children situations, where a high repeat rate may mean that kids have nowhere but the library to go after school. Regardless, the number of repeat customers, as well as overall attendance, should be collected as strong evidence of program use. The library may also decide to collect data on which grades and schools the homework-center participants attend. Not only do these statistics indicate whether specific groups are being reached, but they may also help in targeting publicity campaigns.

Some libraries collect data on which materials and resources are used in conjunction with the homework center. Books used in the library after school may be recorded to indicate subject interests, as well as usage patterns. At two California libraries, the library cards of homework-center participants are encoded to take inventory of the materials they check out. In other libraries, homework-related Internet use is tracked to justify the need for computers in the homework center.

Homework-related reference questions may also be tallied to establish how well the library's collection meets the needs of students. At the Foster City Library, in California, the site coordinator keeps a log of all subject areas requested by homework-center participants. Librarians may opt to use a "homework fill rate" form, which not only records specific titles and subjects, but also whether the student was able to find the desired items on the shelf. A low "fill rate" may indicate a need to review the library's collection in light of local curricula.

Homework-center service hours, as well as the number of hours worked by volunteer helpers, are also tallied to record the scope of the program and the extent of the community's involvement. Repeat pairings between a particular mentor and a student may indicate the growth of a successful working relationship. On the other hand, a large student-to-helper ratio may validate the need for more homework assistants.

Assessing Quality

Many libraries assess the effectiveness of their homework centers simply through observation and anecdotal evidence. For these programs, success is measured by the number of smiles that greet the homework-center staff every day or by the look of comprehension that replaces a child's quizzical frown. At one library, the administrator knew she had reached an important benchmark when a fourth-grade teacher came in to witness for herself the homework program her students had praised so highly.

Anecdotes are a powerful way of humanizing quantitative data. Stories of immigrant teens learning English thanks to the patience and perseverance of homework tutors at the Minneapolis Public Library go a long way toward illustrating the quality of that program. Yet qualitative data are even more meaningful when collected through formal means, such as staff reports, surveys, or focus groups. At the Houston Public Library, ASPIRE (After School Programs Inspire Reading Enrichment) staff are required to file a monthly report with at least one anecdotal "success story." Likewise, in Monterey County, library staff are encouraged to share comments, news, and ideas as part of their monthly homework-center evaluation.

Surveys have been successfully utilized at several libraries to assess the satisfaction of homework-center patrons and staff (*see* appendix K for examples). Twice a year, a postcard survey is mailed to Tucson-area students, parents, and teachers to discern if the library's homework-assistance program has resulted in either a change of attitude toward school or an improvement in course grades. At the Garfield Park Library in Santa Cruz, California, a survey of homework-center users was administered via the library's Internet home page.

In Oakland, feedback about the PASS! program is collected annually from students, teachers, parents, homework mentors, and library staff. Mentors and staff alike are asked for their input on ways to improve the program, while kids and their parents are queried about the impact of PASS! on schoolwork and reading ability. In addition, teachers are surveyed about their familiarity with PASS! and other local homework-assistance programs. At the San Jose and Brooklyn public libraries, students are asked why they visit the homework program—for instance, to prepare for a test, to have a quiet place to study, to use books and materials not available at home, or "because my mother made me." Elsewhere staff are required to record every homework transaction, noting such information as the student's question, how the question was handled, whether the student was satisfied, and which materials were not available.

In Sacramento, a telephone survey is conducted once a year by a consultant who personally interviews parents and teachers about the effectiveness of the library's after-school program. Parents are asked if, as a result of attending the homework center, the child

- is more confident about doing homework,

- does better in school,

- uses the library more, or

- reads more.

Teachers, on the other hand, are asked if they have noticed an improvement in the

- completion rate of the student's homework,

- student's attitude toward school,

- student's attendance, and

- student's reading and math grades.

Although the data collected this way are revealing, library staff note that telephone surveys can be difficult to administer in low-income areas. Language barriers are often an issue, as are the lack of telephones in especially poor neighborhoods.

Besides surveys, focus groups are another effective way of gathering feedback about the library's homework program. A focus group is nothing more than a group interview with some six to twelve people. For instance, students who regularly use the homework center could be asked to meet for fifteen to thirty minutes to evaluate the program and suggest areas for improvement. Focus-group sessions should be conducted by a neutral and, if necessary, bilingual facilitator in a casual environment. Questions should be open-ended to avoid one-word answers. Walter suggests asking kids

- what kinds of homework they do while using the homework center,

- why they use the homework center,

- their impressions of the homework center,

- what they like best about the program, and

- how the program can be improved.

In Oakland, three separate sets of successful focus-group sessions were held with PASS! participants, mentors, and parents (*see* appendix L for lists of focus-group questions). Efforts were made to ease the interview process by providing refreshments, incentives, translators, reimbursement for transportation, and child care.

Summary

Because funders need "hard data" to justify financial support, librarians must find a way to evaluate the effectiveness of their homework programs. Assessment is also helpful in determining whether the program is working and in identifying the need for improvement or change. By using assessment methods such as attendance records, homework fill rates, surveys, and focus groups, evaluators should be able to discern whether the homework program is accomplishing its stated goals and objectives, reaching its target population, and having an impact on the lives of the students served. The evaluator should also be able to decipher the quantity and quality of the assistance offered as part of the program.

Model Homework Programs

PROGRAM

Quest

LIBRARY

East Palo Alto Branch, San Mateo County Libraries, East Palo Alto, California

CONTACT PERSON

Jeanine Asche, Youth Services Program Manager
650/312-5263
aschej@pls.lib.ca.us

HOURS

Monday through Friday, 3:00 to 6:00 P.M.

FUNDING SOURCE

Originally financed by county funds earmarked for "prevention programs," the homework center is now part of the library's regular budget.

STAFFING

Three part-time tutors, one of whom coordinates the program as "lead tutor"

TARGET POPULATION

At-risk youth, ages thirteen to seventeen. Most of the kids who participate are Latino teenagers.

PURPOSE

The program provides learning and mentoring support to young adults lacking basic educational and language-development skills.

SPECIAL FEATURES

Quest is run like a club, to which students must apply before being considered for membership. Acceptance into the homework club is postponed if the tutors feel the student has not demonstrated enough maturity to make a long-term commitment. Students earn points for regular attendance and are penalized for inappropriate behavior. Points are posted on a bulletin board in the homework-center area. Once the students have earned a requisite number of points, they are then invited to participate in weekend "field trips" to various cultural and educational events in the local area.

The homework area is located in the front portion of the library within clear view of staff and patrons. Orange-rubber road "cones" are brought out at 3:00 P.M. to delineate the "homework only" zone. To use one of the handful of tables within this prestigious coned-off area, students must be working on school assignments; otherwise, they will be asked to sit elsewhere in the library. Tutors help the kids with their homework. Non-Quest members may also seek homework assistance on a drop-in basis only.

Besides providing homework assistance, the tutors also serve as positive role models by mentoring the students and encouraging educational pursuits. On the day I visited, one of the students just learned that she had been accepted into Stanford University's Upward Bound program, thanks to the support received from the homework-center staff. The lead tutor is a young Latino community-college professor whom the kids obviously admire and respect. The importance of a good education is constantly emphasized.

PROGRAM

Castroville Library Homework Center

LIBRARY

Castroville Library, Monterey County Free Libraries, Castroville, California

CONTACT PERSONS

Shirley Dawson, Branch Librarian
Sally Childs, Homework Center Coordinator
831/633-2829
mands@redshift.com

HOURS

Tuesday, 3:00 to 7:00 P.M.; Wednesday, 3:00 to 6:00 P.M.; and Thursday, 3:00 to 7:00 P.M.

FUNDING SOURCE

All twelve of the county library's Homework Centers are funded by the Foundation for Monterey County Free Libraries.

STAFFING

The part-time Homework Center coordinator runs the program under the supervision of the branch librarian and is assisted by several volunteers.

TARGET POPULATION

Although students of all ages are welcome to use the Homework Center, the program has been most popular with middle- and high-school students.

PURPOSE

The Homework Center welcomes young people into the world of libraries by offering them assistance with their information needs and homework assignments.

SPECIAL FEATURES

Three afternoons a week, the entire Castroville Library becomes an after-school homework center as teenagers descend on the small branch requesting homework assistance and a quiet place to study. To encourage the kids to ask for help, the Homework Center coordinator greets every student and asks what projects each one is working on. The library's two Internet stations are a big draw, as are the three networked computers that provide access to Social Issues Resources Series (SIRS), CD-ROM encyclopedias in English and Spanish, a magazine index, and Current Biography. Because many of these kids do not have computers at home, they also make good use of several word processors that were donated to the library specifically for typing school assignments.

Volunteer homework helpers are recruited from the California State University campus in nearby Monterey Bay. As part of the university curriculum, CSUMB students are required to provide thirty hours of community service while taking "service learning" classes. In addition, computer science students are required to work as community "technology tutors." Not only do these university students offer experienced homework assistance, but they serve as powerful role models for kids who never before dreamed of attending college themselves. Often, the older students spend as much time answering questions about college as they do helping the younger kids with homework.

College preparation is an important component of the Castroville program. The local high-school migrant-education counselor often uses the library for after-school tutoring and Scholastic Aptitude Test (SAT) study sessions. Every January, the Homework Center coordinator and the migrant-education counselor invite college financial aid advisors to the library to explain the financial aid process and help students fill out the necessary forms.

In 1999, the Castroville Library Homework Center received YALSA's award for Excellence in Library Services to Young Adults.

PROGRAM

PASS! (Partners for Achieving School Success)

LIBRARY

César E. Chávez Branch Library, Oakland Public Library, Oakland, California

CONTACT PERSON

Patricia M. Wong, Library Program Coordinator
  for Children's Services
510/238-6706
pwong@oaklandnet.com

HOURS

Monday to Thursday, 3:20 to 5:20 P.M.

FUNDING SOURCES

The PASS! program, which operates in ten Oakland branch libraries, is supported through private donations raised by the Oakland Public Library Foundation and the Friends of the Oakland Public Library.

STAFFING

The part-time PASS! site coordinator runs the program under the supervision of the children's librarian. Homework assistance is provided by teen workers.

TARGET POPULATION

Although the program is targeted at second- to ninth-graders, the César E. Chávez homework center is used primarily by elementary-school children.

PURPOSE

Among the program's goals are to help at-risk youth to succeed in school by completing homework assignments and developing library skills and to provide high-school students with meaningful employment in the library, job training, and extensive youth-leadership-development experiences.

SPECIAL FEATURES

After-school homework assistance is provided four days a week in the children's area of the César E. Chávez Branch Library. Despite cramped quarters, the children work diligently together at small tables, while adults sit nearby reading books and magazines or chatting in low tones. Hanging from the ceiling is a sign that requests, "Por favor baje la voz—otras personas quieren leer!!!" ("Please lower your voice—others want to read!!!") The collection is equally represented by English- and Spanish-language materials. Homework assistance is provided in both languages. A core collection of ready-reference materials is wheeled out on a cart during PASS! hours. Two computers are available specifically for working on homework assignments.

The César E. Chávez homework-assistance program is so popular that kids are scheduled on alternating days. A list of names and assigned days is posted in the children's area. To participate in the program, children must come ready to work on school assignments. Exhibiting polite behavior, cooperating, and helping others to complete their homework are rewarded through a "Student of the Week" ceremony where kids receive a certificate and small gift, courtesy of the library staff. Names of the celebrated students are then posted on a bulletin board in the children's area.

Homework assistance is provided by honor-roll high-school students hired through an agency called the Youth Employment Partnership, Inc. (YEP). YEP and the library share responsibility for training the homework "mentors." As part of their compensation, the high schoolers also attend workshops on how to write résumés and apply for college. Teen mentors are recognized at a year-end party.

PASS! received YALSA's Excellence in Library Services to Young Adults award in 1999.

PROGRAM

Homework Pals

LIBRARY

Monterey Public Library, Monterey, California

CONTACT PERSON

Dina Stansbury, Homework Pals Program Coordinator
831/646-5604
stansbur@ci.monterey.ca.us

HOURS

Site specific, 2:15 to 5:30 P.M., Monday to Thursday

FUNDING SOURCE

The program is funded by the library and was recently expanded, thanks to a two-year grant from the Monterey Rotary Club.

STAFFING

A full-time coordinator recruits, trains, and supervises volunteer Homework Pals. The actual homework assistance is provided by volunteers.

TARGET POPULATION

Kindergartners to fifth-graders enrolled in after-school day-care programs at elementary schools in the city of Monterey

PURPOSE

Volunteers give children individual attention to help them complete challenging school-related tasks and discover or rediscover the joy of reading.

SPECIAL FEATURES

Homework Pals exists thanks to a unique partnership between the library, the Monterey Peninsula Unified School District, and after-school day-care providers. The coordinator oversees the program, which provides homework assistance as part of after-school day care at seven elementary schools and one recreational site. The library's bookmobile makes regular stops at several Homework Pals locations, and the youth-services manager conducts monthly after-school story times at each of the sites. The library, in conjunction with the school district, sponsors an annual homework-help-related workshop for parents and the community.

Although teachers and parents may recommend that particular students participate, Homework Pals is a student-driven program. Children sign up to work with Homework Pals on a daily basis for a variety of reasons. Day-care-center staff assign each child to a Homework Pal, with whom he or she works one-on-one. Sessions vary from ten minutes to an hour, depending on need. All of the children in the after-school day-care program are eligible to participate, and the Homework Pals work with any child who signs up.

Homework Pal recruitment is ongoing, with brochures and flyers circulated throughout the year. In addition, two active recruitment drives occur in August and January. Publicity appears via the radio, television, community calendar, newsletters, and the newspaper. Interested people receive information packets; are privately interviewed, fingerprinted, and tested for tuberculosis; and agree to a sheriff's background check. A six-hour orientation is followed by monthly training. Volunteers range in age from sixteen to eighty-five and come from all types of backgrounds. All are motivated by a desire to work with kids.

PROGRAM

Math Homework Help

LIBRARY

Monroe County Public Library, Bloomington, Indiana

CONTACT PERSON

Dana Burton, Youth Services Librarian
812/349-3050
dburton@monroe.lib.in.us

HOURS

Monday, 7:00 to 9:00 P.M.

FUNDING SOURCES

Expenses are shared by the library, McDonald's restaurants, the Monroe County Education Association, and the Monroe County Community School Corporation.

STAFFING

The tutor coordinator, who reports to the youth-services librarian, recruits and schedules several volunteer tutors.

TARGET POPULATION

Seventh- to twelfth-grade students needing help with math assignments

PURPOSE

In response to a need expressed by young adults, the library offers after-school math assistance one night a week. Tutoring is not long term but rather focused on more immediate math problems.

SPECIAL FEATURES

Every Monday evening during the school year, the library's Teen Program room is turned into a tutoring center for middle- and high-school students needing math help. The program is organized by a teacher who not only provides homework assistance, but also recruits and schedules a team of volunteer tutors. The tutors, who come from nearby businesses and Indiana University, have extensive backgrounds in mathematics as well as patience enough to work with kids. Younger students are also recruited as peer tutors because many teens feel less intimidated working with kids their own age.

The tutor coordinator has marvelous rapport with the students. Never does he directly give them the answers, preferring instead to pose math problems in a way that encourages the students to discover the solutions themselves. The atmosphere is casual and non-threatening, with tables of students helping each other with their homework. Food is allowed. Because the Teen Program room is visible to all who walk past, other teenage library users often "cruise" by to see who is inside.

Math Homework Help has evolved into a community partnership. The library hosts the Monday-night session, while the local McDonald's restaurant hosts a Wednesday-night session. Each site's tutor coordinator is paid an hourly wage. McDonald's funds the Wednesday coordinator, and the library, the teacher's union (Monroe County Education Association), and the Monroe County Community School Corporation fund the Monday-night coordinator. Math Homework Help is advertised as one program with two sites. The youth-services librarian creates flyers and coordinates publicity. McDonald's pays for printing and places flyers in take-out orders once a semester.

PROGRAM

Homework Help

LIBRARY

Allen County Public Library, Fort Wayne, Indiana

CONTACT PERSON

Suzanne Murray, Librarian and Homework Help
  Coordinator
219/421-1200, ext. 2452
smurray@acpl.lib.in.us

HOURS

Tuesday to Thursday, 6:30 to 8:30 P.M.

FUNDING SOURCE

The Friends of the Library purchased the computers
and initially funded the Homework Help coordinator's
salary. The program, including the coordinator's salary,
is now totally funded by the library.

STAFFING

A part-time young adult librarian coordinates the Homework Help program and supervises a team of volunteers.

TARGET POPULATION

Sixth- to twelfth-graders

PURPOSE

The program provides drop-in, one-on-one homework
assistance to middle- and high-school students three
nights a week.

SPECIAL FEATURES

The library began its Homework Help program in
response to a Citizen's Panel on Violence and Youth. To
help students succeed, the library started offering after-
school homework assistance specifically for teens. The
Friends of the Library purchased three computers for
homework use only. Initially, a part-time coordinator
was hired to run the program during weeknights. That
task now falls to the part-time young adult librarian.
The library's volunteer-services manager recruits Homework Helpers through local companies and community
agencies. Although many of the volunteers are motivated by a love of mathematics, all helpers share a
desire to help kids succeed.

The library's expansive young adults section is the
site of the Homework Help program. Tutoring takes
place on a table in the center of the room. Students
may approach staff, who will then refer the person to an
available volunteer, or may go directly to the volunteer
if no one else is waiting. The helper then assists the
student with that evening's homework problem(s). All
homework subjects are tackled.

Kids come in on their own or are brought in by
their parents. In either case, the kids feel a definite
need to improve their grades. Although no formal
assessment occurs, the helpers do notice an improvement in the students' skills. The ratio between volunteers and kids is kept purposely low (up to eight students
a night) to maximize individualized attention.

PROGRAM

Homework Cafe

LIBRARY

Northfield Public Library, Northfield, Minnesota

CONTACT PERSON

Leesa Wisdorf, Children's and Young Adult Librarian
507/645-6606
LEESA@selco.lib.mn.us

HOURS

Wednesday, 3:00 to 5:00 P.M.

FUNDING SOURCE

The program is considered part of the library's regular service and, therefore, is absorbed into the children's and young adult budget. The snack bar, which is sponsored by the library's Teen Advisory Board, is self-supporting.

STAFFING

The children's and young adult librarians oversee the program. Volunteers provide homework assistance. One volunteer is responsible for scheduling the others.

TARGET POPULATION

Middle-school students

PURPOSE

The Homework Cafe provides a safe place for teens and preteens to go and unwind after school. Homework assistance is also provided.

SPECIAL FEATURES

One afternoon a week, the library's community room is turned into the Homework Cafe, where kids can buy snacks and get homework help from college-student volunteers. The snack bar, which provides cookies, candies, fruit, and various beverages, is run and staffed by the Teen Advisory Board. Eating is allowed in the community room but prohibited in other parts of the library.

Although Northfield is a small, midwestern town, it is home to two prestigious private educational institutions, Carleton College and St. Olaf College. Because volunteerism is emphasized as part of both schools' curricula, recruitment of after-school homework tutors is fairly easy. The tutors' schedules are coordinated by a volunteer, who communicates with the others primarily through e-mail. Homework helpers are rewarded through staff letters of recommendation, recognition in the library's newsletter, and gift certificates to the campus bookstore or local bagel shop. Homework assistance is provided in all subject areas.

Northfield's two children's and young adult librarians take turns overseeing the Homework Cafe. Duties include setting up the community-room's tables and chairs and remaining available during Homework Cafe hours. Despite a shoestring budget, this program attracts up to thirty kids a week, especially during the cold winter months.

PROGRAM

Math Peer Tutoring Center

LIBRARY

Brooklyn Public Library, Brooklyn, New York

CONTACT PERSON

Douglas Wooley, librarian
718/230-2119
d.wooley@brooklynpubliclibrary.org

HOURS

Monday, 4:00 to 5:00 P.M.

FUNDING SOURCE

This program is considered part of the library's regular service and, therefore, is included in the Youth Services budget.

STAFFING

The young adult services librarian oversees the program. High-school volunteers provide the homework assistance.

TARGET POPULATION

Although the program was developed specifically for seventh- to twelfth-grade students, younger kids and GED students have also participated.

PURPOSE

This drop-in program offers free one-on-one help with math homework.

SPECIAL FEATURES

Once a week, the central library's auditorium is turned into a tutoring center where high-school students help peers and younger kids with their math homework. The tutors are recruited through the library's Book Buddy program, as well as through local high-school math departments. The qualifications of all tutor applicants are confirmed with the student's mathematics teacher. An agreement between the teen tutor, the school, and the library is signed by all three parties. Parents must also give permission before their child can work as a tutor. Although an assortment of tutors from the various schools is preferred, staff have found that teen volunteers will make a longer commitment if they can work alongside friends or classmates. Staff have also found that communication with math teachers is essential.

Flyers describing the program are sent to local schools and are posted in the library's young adult section. The most effective advertisement, however, is an announcement over the library's loudspeaker five minutes before the tutoring center opens. Besides math assistance, the library provides such homework supplies as graph paper, pencils, calculators, rulers, and protractors. Textbooks are also made available. The young adult librarian is present at all times to monitor activities and make referrals.

In 1997, the Math Peer Tutoring Center received a YALSA Excellence in Library Services to Young Adults award.

PROGRAM

Homework Help

LIBRARY

New Rochelle Public Library, New Rochelle, New York

CONTACT PERSON

Kathleen Cronin, Head of Children's Services
914/632-7878
kcronin@wls.lib.ny.us

HOURS

Monday to Thursday, 3:30 to 5:30 P.M.

FUNDING SOURCES

Reader's Digest was initially a major contributor to the Homework Help program, which started as part of the Tall Tree Initiative, the library's after-school program. Today the program is sponsored by the New Rochelle Board of Education, who pays for the Teacher in the Library service. Federal America Reads and Community Development Block Grant (CDBG) programs also provide money to hire tutors.

STAFFING

Homework Help is run by the library's head of children's services. Homework assistance is provided by a team of America Reads teens, library staff, and two teachers who work part-time for the library.

TARGET POPULATION

Kindergartners to fifth-graders

PURPOSE

Homework Help continues to maintain all the Tall Tree Initiative goals for children, which include to become better and more enthusiastic readers, develop strong basic academic skills, and become competent and confident creators and users of information.

SPECIAL FEATURES

During the academic year, teachers from nearby school districts are hired to provide after-school homework assistance in the children's section of the New Rochelle Public Library. This service, called Teacher in the Library, is but one part of a larger program that strives to strengthen ties between the library and local schools. Other related programs include Librarian in the School, where public librarians visit local schools to teach kids how to use print and electronic sources; Children as Researchers, where students complete a project designed to demonstrate mastery of the research process; Ready, Set, Grow, a reading program; and Family Nights at the Library.

The teachers who participate in Teacher in the Library are motivated by a desire to see kids complete their homework and, therefore, succeed in school. Because these teachers tend to live locally, they have a keen appreciation of how the Tall Tree Initiative benefits the community as a whole. Supplemental homework assistance is provided by America Reads teens, who have demonstrated scholastic ability and share a willingness to serve others. Because homework assistance has been fully integrated into the library's mission, the library staff also play an active role in helping kids after school.

Two computer stations are located in the center of the children's room. A local area network (LAN) provides access to fourteen educational programs for after-school use. The teacher-tutors also make good use of flash cards and other interactive tools, such as an abacus, to help kids build math and language skills.

In conjunction with a local Boys Club and the federal Housing Authority, the library also oversees a separate homework center in a nearby low-income housing project. A bilingual library aide, whose salary is funded through CDBG monies, provides assistance.

71

PROGRAM

Homework Help Center

LIBRARY

Woodrow Wilson Community Library, Fairfax County Public Library, Falls Church, Virginia

CONTACT PERSON

Bonnie Worcester, Branch Manager
703/820-8774
bonnie.worcester@co.fairfax.va.us

HOURS

Monday to Wednesday, 3:30 to 5:00 P.M.

FUNDING SOURCES

The center was founded in partnership with the Virginia Cooperative Extension/4-H. The Friends of the Library and local church groups provide after-school snacks and supplies. The library absorbs all overhead expenses associated with staffing and maintaining the facility.

STAFFING

Although the branch manager is ultimately responsible for the program, she does delegate the day-to-day operation to a children's librarian who serves as Homework Help Center coordinator. Volunteer tutors provide homework assistance.

TARGET POPULATION

The multilingual students of the kindergarten-through-fifth-grade elementary school next door are the primary users of the program. Students from a nearby middle school also attend.

PURPOSE

The program provides after-school homework assistance to students from various cultural backgrounds.

SPECIAL FEATURES

Prompted by a need to control a severe unattended-children problem caused by students from the nearby elementary school, the Woodrow Wilson Community Library initially teamed up with various local agencies to help focus the kids' energies on doing homework after school. Homework assistance is provided in the library's community room by volunteers and the children's librarian. Rules of conduct are posted on the community-room wall. Once the children have completed their homework, they are encouraged to either read to each other or fill out educational work sheets. Each child has a folder where works-in-progress and completed sheets are kept. Occasionally, guest speakers from law enforcement and the health professions make presentations. Snacks are served each day to all the children and volunteers. Because the children represent cultures from some twenty-six countries, staff are particularly sensitive to dietary restraints and ethnic traditions.

Volunteers are recruited from the local community, Americorps, and the high school. Each volunteer wears a blue library-logo button and is called by her or his first name. Library staff maintain an active dialogue with the principals and staff of nearby schools to ensure the volunteer support is meeting the students' needs. A year-end party is held for the students and volunteers.

Needs Assessment Tools

Focus Group Protocol
Teen Library and Non-Library Users
2/4/99

Reminder: The conversation that these questions hope to stimulate is intended to help us better understand what teens want from and can offer to public libraries. Please express yourselves honestly. Everything you say will be reported anonymously and compiled with the responses of others.

1. What do you typically do after school? (round robin)

   PROBES

      • Where do you go (e.g., home, school, library, other youth programs)?

      • What do you do (e.g., TV, computer, homework, friends, work for money, volunteer, read)?

      • Why do you do this?

   Okay, now that I know what you do after school, and (some of you do/don't go to the library . . .), I'd like to hear what's needed to get teens to use the library more often, to attend its programs and make it a place that's fun and helpful for you and your friends. So let's suppose for a few minutes that I am Jerry Brown, our new mayor, and let's also suppose that you are my advisors, helping me make Oakland a better place, and I ask:

2. What could the library offer to you and your friends to make it a place you'd want to come to more often?

   PROBES

      • What's needed that's not there (e.g., snacks, space to talk with friends, homework help, school supplies, computer help, job opportunities, practice/performance space)?

      • Are there things about the library that you don't like, that if changed perhaps you'd want to come more often (e.g., hours, rules, computer time, transportation problems)?

3. Let's talk about things that you read when you aren't doing school work. What kinds of things do you read (e.g., books, magazines, comics, webpages/E-mails, fotonovelas)?

   PROBES

      • Do you go to the library to get reading materials?

      • Where else do you get reading materials?

4. Now let's talk about computers. We're guessing they're a big reason teens come to the library. Have you had a chance to learn how to use the Internet yet?

   PROBES

   - Where do you use computers and do you like using them there?
   - What's needed, if anything, to give you more of a chance to use computers (e.g., training, on-demand help, better access to computers, more time on computers, better hard/software)?
   - Who do you currently get help from and who would you want to get help from (e.g., peers)?

5. Earlier you mention that after school you_____.
   Let's talk now about where and when you do your homework.

   PROBES

   - When do you typically do it?
   - Where (e.g., home, at a friend's home, library, school)?
   - Why/why not use the library?
   - If you need help, where do you get it and from whom? Is this good enough?

6. The library's also trying to give teens opportunities at libraries to help their communities and to do something meaningful when not at school. How do you think teens like you and your friends could be involved? What kinds of things could you do (e.g., tutor, teach ESL, teach other languages, assist others on the computer, teach children [puppetry, storytelling], advise library staff about policies and selection of materials, plan special events [read-a-thon, workshops])?

   PROBES

   - What could teens get out of doing these kinds of things (e.g., leadership and job skills, college and work experience)?
   - What could the library gain from having this kind of teen involvement?

7. Comments

SOURCE: WestEd, Oakland. *The Oakland Public Library as a Partner in Youth Development: An Evaluation of PASS! and a Needs-Wants Assessment of Library-Linked Youth Development Programs.* Staff report. June 1999.

Homework

Alert Center

Homework Alert Center Questionnaire

Dear Students,

Would you please take a moment, as a select sample, to fill out the following questionnaire? Your thoughtful answers will help us design Homework Alert Centers for the Corvallis–Benton County Public Library. These centers will be a starting point for you when you come to the library to complete assignments. Completed questionnaires may be returned to your teacher to forward to the CIMC in care of Jan Deardorff. Please complete by Nov. 10. Thank you!

1. Please list basic references that you use, such as encyclopedias, etc.:

2. Would you use trained volunteer mentors for reference help if available?

3. What hours are you most likely to use the library for homework?

    (new hours are Mon.-Fri. 9-9, Sat. 9-6 and Sun. 12-6)

4. What subject areas do you study at the library?

5. Would you like the use of a typewriter/word processor?

6. Do you know how to search for references using the on-line catalogue?

7. Would you please recommend any study aids you feel would be useful such as computer software, CD roms, magazines, etc.:

8. What office supplies would be useful such as pencils, scissors, tape, etc.?

9. Are there other ways that the Public Library could assist you in completing assignments?

Homework Alert Center Questionnaire

Dear Teachers,

Would you please take a moment, as a select sample, to fill out the following questionnaire? Your thoughtful answers will help us design Homework Alert Centers for the Corvallis-Benton County Public Library. These centers will enable your students to successfully complete their assignments while learning about the many and various resources of the library. Completed forms may be returned by district courier to Kim Thompson in care of Jan Deardorff at the CIMC. Please return by Nov. 10. Thank you!

1. Please list basic reference materials you feel should be in the center:

2. Please list basic office supplies you feel should be available:

3. What hours do you think your students would most likely use the center?

   (new hours are Mon.-Fri. 9-9, Sat. 9-6 and Sun. 12-6)

4. Would your students use the services of trained volunteer mentors as reference aides?

5. What subject areas are students most likely to study in the library?

6. Can you recommend CD roms, computer hardware or software, or other study aids?

7. Other suggestions: (use the back if necessary)

Homework-Center Goals and Objectives

Homework Pals
A homework and academic enrichment program
of the Monterey Public Library

HOMEWORK PALS

Mission

Working cooperatively with the City and local schools, Homework Pals offers homework assistance and academic enrichment activities to students after regular school hours at after school centers

Goals

- Create a program in which volunteers will:

    Become partners with students to help them successfully complete their homework at their after school facility

    Introduce students to library resources and help them learn how to use those resources

    Become reading partners who will read with students on a one-to-one basis, in order to motivate students to additional reading

- Provide enrichment programs for parents, students and teachers to help students succeed in school

- Provide opportunities for greater cooperation between the Monterey Peninsula Unified School District and the City of Monterey

---

SOURCE: Homework Pal Training Manual, November 1996.

SCHOOLINKS HOMEWORK CENTER

The SchooLinks Homework Center program of the Ojai Valley Library Foundation is a public-private partnership designed to help students of all ages gain lifelong information-gathering and learning skills. The electronically equipped centers, which are based at the three public libraries in the Ojai Valley, also offer one-on-one homework assistance and tutoring to help students succeed in school.

Objectives

The SchooLinks Homework Centers are designed to benefit young people by:

- Promoting information literacy through training in the use of both print and electronic information resources at the library.

- Enabling young people to become lifelong independent problem-solvers.

- Furnishing positive role models and opportunities for constructive extra-curricular activities in a safe and stimulating environment.

- Building a foundation for resource-sharing between the community's public libraries and local schools.

- Boosting academic achievement.

SOURCE: SchooLinks Homework Centers Program Evaluation, 1997–98, pp. 1–2.

Sacramento Public Library

GOAL AND OBJECTIVES
OF THE PILOT HOMEWORK CENTER

Goal

The goal of the Pilot Homework Center is to strengthen after school use of the public library by youth from kindergarten through eighth grade by providing organized programs. Studies have shown that this is an age when children are most impressionable and can be reached before they turn to drugs, alcohol and gangs and drop out of school. It is also the age that provides the basis for lifelong learning.

Objectives

The Homework Center will achieve this goal through a program that combines the efforts of the Library with parents, schools, and other community resources and expands library resources and group activities at the library. Specifically, the objectives are to

- Enroll 100 youth at risk from three schools near the King Regional Library and sustain their use of the library throughout the school year.

- Provide these youth with a personal orientation to the library, build their skills in using library resources, and help them find materials and information to complete their school assignments.

- Foster peer support among the program participants through weekly group activities related to interests, reading abilities, and skill levels.

- Install personal computers with interactive software and access to the Internet, train students in the use of these programs, and show how they can be used to satisfy educational needs. The Library will provide software that includes geography, math, social studies, language, reading and learning skills that supplement educational activities.

- Involve teachers from the three schools in order to target youth at risk and identify their needs, and track progress of students during the school year.

- Involve the parents of the students in order to target student needs and gain support and reinforcement from home as well as school.

SOURCE: Sacramento Public Library Homework Center for Youth at Risk Pilot, pp. 2–3.

Homework-Helper Recruitment Flyers

San Mateo County Library

HOMEWORK CENTER TUTOR

(Part-Time Non-Benefitted)

$14.82/hour

SAN MATEO COUNTY is looking for a tutor to work in the Foster City Library Homework Center. The position is part-time Monday-Thursday 3:30-6 and Tuesday-Wednesday 7:00-9:00 when school is in session. The homework center is a joint project of the SMUHS District, SMFC Elementary School district, San Mateo County Library and Friends of the Foster City Library. The primary purpose of the program is to provide learning support for middle and high school students by assisting students with their homework.

As a tutor, you will:

- Assist students with homework in a wide variety of subjects

- Act as a liaison between the library and teachers to clarify and secure resources for assignments

- Work in partnership with reference/children's librarians to assist students in their homework

- Instruct students in the use of the on-line catalog, magazine index, Internet and CD-ROM resources

- Work with Branch Manager in creating policies and procedures for the Center

- Facilitate a productive environment for learning

- Assist/tutor individual students in their barriers to learning

This position requires a person with the following knowledge and skills: well organized; a team player; able to communicate effectively with teens, parents, school and library personnel; capable of writing in a clear, concise manner; sensitive to diverse cultures and population; computer and Internet literacy; flexible and self-directed.

Experience: One or more years working with middle to high school age students tutoring/teaching.

Education: One year or more college training or equivalent experience.

Brooklyn
Public
Library

Dear Math Teacher,

The Central Library Youth Services Division of the Brooklyn Public Library would like to invite 11th and 12th grade students excelling in mathematics to participate in our Math Peer Tutoring Center beginning in the fall of 2000. This award winning program begins its sixth year in September.

Students recommended as peer tutors are interviewed at the Library; those chosen to be tutors must attend a one hour orientation in mid-September. The tutors report to the Library on Monday, 4–5 P.M., when the public high schools are in session. They provide one on one tutoring to 7th through 12th graders who need help with mathematics. We look for tutors who have strong math and communication skills as well as good attendance and punctuality.

The tutoring sessions are supervised by a librarian at all times. Tutors usually reinforce and strengthen their own math skills as they explain problems to others. In addition, tutors who complete the school year receive a certificate of recognition signed by the Executive Director of the Library, Martín Gómez, as well as a party and token gift. Many schools also give tutors community service credit for their efforts. The peer tutor experience is also impressive on resumés and college applications. We are proud of this very successful program, and hope you can recommend some interested juniors and seniors to participate in next year's Math Peer Tutoring Center.

Interested students can apply at the Central Library Youth Services Division. Thank you for your time and consideration.

Sincerely,

Volunteer Opportunity
Homework Help Program

January 2000

What? In its seventh semester, this exciting program offers homework help to middle and high school students on a drop-in basis. Volunteer homework helpers will provide one-on-one instruction to students trying to understand and complete their homework. Math is the primary subject area with science, social studies, or English as secondary.

Why? A recent survey showed that 81% of polled Allen County teens need homework help, with 40% of them needing help weekly. Math was identified as the number one problem, and the majority of those polled reported they welcome a drop-in homework help program from the library.

How? A Young Adults' Librarian in the Young Adults' Services Area will train and supervise a core of volunteer homework helpers. Drop-in homework help sessions are offered 3 times per week using this core of volunteers. In addition to volunteer helpers, special computers with learning software will be available to students, for use independently or with their volunteer helper.

Where? Young Adults' Services department, Main Library, Allen County Public Library, 900 Webster Street, Fort Wayne.

When? The Homework Help Center is open during the school year on Tuesdays through Thursdays from 6:30-8:30 p.m.

Who? We're looking for people with strong backgrounds in middle and secondary school subjects such as math, science, social studies, and English; people who care about kids and want to help them succeed academically; and people willing to give 2 hours per week for at least one semester.

You? Interested? Need more information? Contact Sandy Screeton, Allen County Public Library Volunteer Services Manager, at (219) 421-1233, or e-mail at sscreeton@acpl.lib.in.us.

Allen County Public Library • 900 Webster St. • PO Box 2270 • Fort Wayne, IN • 46801-2270

Be a Tutor!

Looking for a community service opportunity or need some teaching experience? The Tigard Library is looking for dedicated and enthusiastic volunteers, just 2 hours per week, for its after school Homework Center.

Where: Tigard Public Library

When: Mondays, Tuesdays, or Wednesdays from 4:00 – 6:00 p.m., starting October 4, 1999 through May 2000.

Who: Volunteers committed to tutoring middle school and high school students.

What: Be prepared to help with a variety of assignments, from English papers to chemistry problems.

Why: Help students tackle their homework, gain valuable experience, and have fun.

Questions?

Contact Marin Younker, Young Adult Services Librarian, or Trish Stormont, Volunteer Coordinator, at (503) 684-6537 for more information.

Tigard Public Library
13125 SW Hall Blvd.
Tigard, OR 97223
Phone: (503) 684-6537
Fax: (503) 598-7515

Homework-Helper Application Forms

VOLUNTEER APPLICATION

Date:_____

Name:_____

Address:_____
Street   City   Zip

If student, name of school:_____

Emergency contact person:_____
Name   Phone

Age range:

☐   ☐   ☐   ☐   ☐
Under 18   18-25   26-36   37-50   Over 50

Reason for volunteering:_____

_____

Days Available:	Mon.	Tues.	Wed.	Thurs.	Fri.	Sat.
Shift Available:	2-4	2-4	2-4	2-4	2-4	11-1
	4-6	4-6	4-6	4-6	4-6	1-3
	6-8	6-8				3-5

Total hours per week available:_____

Are there any limitations that may restrict your volunteer service?

_____

Thank you for your interest in offering your volunteer
service to the Family Technology Learning Center.

Monterey County Free Libraries

VOLUNTEER REGISTRATION FORM

HOMEWORK CENTERS/STORYTIME

Last Name _____ First Name _____

Street Address _____

City and Zip Code _____

Daytime Phone _____ Evening Phone _____

In case of emergency, please contact:

Name _____ Phone Number _____

EXPERIENCE

Please list previous **work** OR **volunteer** experience with **children/teens,** including **dates, location, organization, ages and description of work.** (continue on back, if needed)

_____

_____

_____

_____

_____

Are you presently employed? _____

Previous work experience, if applicable _____

_____

Special skills, training or interests: (please check all that apply; continue on back)

_____ Storytimes/storytelling   _____ Art projects/Crafts

_____ Math   _____ Reading one-on-one

_____ Bi-lingual   What language(s)? _____

_____ Other _____

Have you ever been convicted of a crime?   _____ yes   _____ no

If yes, this information will be reviewed for job relatedness.

Date: _____

Charge: _____

Place: _____

Action taken: _____

I declare under penalty of perjury that all statements on this application form are true and complete to the best of my knowledge. I understand that false, misleading or incomplete information shall be cause for disqualification.

Signature _____ Date _____

(please complete both sides of application)

AVAILABILITY

I am available to work: _____ Mornings _____ Afternoons

_____ Monday _____ Tuesday _____ Wednesday _____ Thursday

Frequency? _____ times/month _____ times/year

Preferred day(s) and hour(s) _____

How did you hear of this program? _____

_____

_____

_____

What do you hope to gain from this program? _____

_____

_____

_____

_____

Experience, employment or special skills, continued:

_____

_____

_____

_____

_____

_____

_____

VOLUNTEER APPLICATION FORM
Allen County Public Library
900 Webster St.   P.O. Box 2270 . Ft. Wayne, IN 46801-2270
(219) 421-1233

Directions: Complete each section **on both sides**. Please print clearly. If you are aged 11 - 17, a parent or guardian's signature is required.

Last Name: _____ First Name: _____ Middle Initial: _____

Street Address: _____

City/State: _____ Zip: _____

Phone: (H) _____ (W): _____ (E-mail): _____

Month and Day of Birth: ___/___

Education: Current School: _____ Highest grade completed: _____

School Name:	Degree:	Major:	Year:
_____	_____	_____	_____
_____	_____	_____	_____
_____	_____	_____	_____

Languages you speak other than English: _____

Current Employment (or most recent if not currently employed):

Are you currently employed? Yes_____   No_____   Part-time_____   Full-time_____   Retired_____

Employer: _____ Occupation/Title: _____

Duties: _____

Emergency Contact Person:

Name: _____ Phone: _____ Relationship: _____

Name: _____ Phone: _____ Relationship: _____

Availability: (check all that apply)

	Monday	Tuesday	Wednesday	Thursday	Friday	Saturday
Mornings						
Afternoons						
Evenings						

Volunteer Experience: Have you had previous volunteer experience? Yes_____ No_____
If so, where and what was your task? _____

_____

(OVER)

87

Interests and Skills: List your skills, hobbies, and interests. _____

_____

What skills do you have that you would like to use at the library? _____

_____

What volunteer activity or activities would you like to pursue at the library? _____

_____

How did you find out about the library's volunteer program? _____

_____

Do you have any physical limitations which we need to accommodate? _____

_____

Is there any other information which will help us place you as a volunteer? _____

_____

References: Please list two references in the space provided below (no family members):

Name: _____ Address: _____ Phone: _____

Name: _____ Address: _____ Phone: _____

Have you been convicted of or pled guilty to a felony or misdemeanor, other than a minor traffic violation? (Conviction or plea will not necessarily disqualify an applicant.) _____ Yes _____ No

If yes, please explain. _____

Please sign below when you have read and understood this statement.

I understand that this information may be disclosed to any party with legal and proper interest, and I release the agency from any liability whatsoever for supplying such information. I grant the agency permission to obtain information from references which I have provided. I certify that the statements made in this volunteer application are true and correct and have been given voluntarily. I understand that misrepresentation of any information may result in termination of my volunteer involvement.

I am volunteering my time for personal reasons. I understand that I will not be paid for my services as a volunteer and I expect no compensation.

Applicant's Signature: _____   _____ Date: _____

My son or daughter has my permission to volunteer at the Allen County Public Library.

Parent/Guardian's Signature: _____ Date: _____
(Required if applicant is under 18)

For Library Use:	
Interview: Date_____	Staff _____
Reference Check _____	Orientation _____
Placement: Agency _____	Position _____
Start Date_____	Schedule _____
Agency Notification _____	Name Tag _____
Parking Tag _____	Computer_____

(5/99)

Corvallis-Benton County Public Library

Homework Alert Center

Mentor Application

The Corvallis-Benton County Public Library will be opening five **Homework Alert Centers** in the four county libraries in January of 1995. Mentors will act as reference guides for students working on assignments. They will be required to 1) Attend two 3-hour training sessions, 2) Volunteer twice a month for two to three hours, 3) Complete the following form to determine qualifications. All information is confidential. *Note: This is not a one-on-one tutoring position.

Name:_____

Address:_____

Phone:_____   _____
        home   work

Educational background:_____

Work experience:_____

Volunteer experience:_____

_____

Special skills :_____

Why do you wish to become a mentor?_____

_____

_____

_____

Will you make a commitment to serve as a mentor until the end of this school year?_____

The **Homework Alert Centers** will probably be staffed Tues, Wed. and Thurs. evenings from 6:30 until 8:30 PM and Sun. 2:30-5:30 PM. Which of those times are you available?

_____

Please list two references:

1. Name:_____Phone:_____

2 Name:_____Phone:_____

Have you ever been convicted of a crime? YES_____NO_____If yes, explain:_____

_____
(exclude minor traffic violations) Conviction does not necessarily disqualify you from further consideration.

Whom should we notify in case of emergency?_____
                                                              Name and phone number

For more information, please contact Kim Thompson, School-Library Liaison, 757-6708

"Bringing People and Information Together"
Corvallis-Benton County Public Library, 645 N.W. Monroe Ave. Corvallis, OR 97330 757-6926

89

Volunteer Application
Multnomah County Library

I would like to be a library volunteer!

Name _____ Day-time phone # _____

Address _____ City/State _____ Zip code _____

Education   Last completed grade _____ **School** _____

Employment   ☐   Not currently employed

Jobs I have had (list most recent first) _____

_____

Volunteer experience   ☐   Never volunteered

List volunteer experience, dates, &   _____
duties

_____

My special interests include _____

Reference _____ **Phone #** _____

If you want to volunteer with children, please list this additional information:

☐ I am willing to have a background check.
☐ I have never been convicted of, and am not currently under indictment for any crime against children.

Social Security number _____ Driver's ID _____ State ____

I would like to volunteer at:
(check all that apply)

☐   Central Library
☐   Title Wave Book Store
☐   Outreach programs
☐   A branch library

List preferred branch(s)

_____

_____

Available hours

☐   Daytime
☐   Evenings
☐   Weekends
☐   Special events

Volunteer work I am interested in doing
(Check all that apply)

☐   Clerical
☐   Computer
☐   Mending Books
☐   Shelf reading/shelving
☐   Working with children
☐   Working with young adults
☐   Book processing
☐   Bringing books to disadvantaged people
☐   Special Events
☐   Reading to elderly
☐   Just want to know my options

Commitment

Most volunteer work requires a commitment of time. Please tell us for how long you would be willing to commit to a volunteer job, assuming you find volunteer work you enjoy.

☐   A week or two
☐   Three months
☐   Six months
☐   Nine months (a school year)
☐   One year
☐   On-going

Signature _____Today's date _____

Please return this application to:
Volunteer Services, Multnomah County Library, 205 NE Russell St, Portland OR 97212-3796

Homework-Helper Contracts

MONTEREY COUNTY FREE LIBRARIES
Volunteer Guidelines
Homework Centers/Storytimes

Welcome! We are delighted that you are joining the volunteer staff of this branch of the Monterey County Free Libraries. By volunteering to work with the children and young people of your community, you are providing educational support and a caring adult role model to each and every child you meet!

As adults, working with children and young people in a public library, we have a responsibility to the children, young people, parents and guardians who use our library services to display respectful, consistent, fair and equitable behaviors. In order to ensure a positive experience for you and the children, we ask that you observe the following guidelines:

1. **All contact between volunteers and children/young people must take place in the library.**
2. **Volunteers should be aware of the child's natural dignity and sense of self. Children are now often taught by parents and teachers not to allow non-family members to touch them; please respect this and do not initiate close contact.**
3. **Any problems with children should be referred to the Homework Center Coordinator or library staff so s/he can help resolve them.**
4. **Volunteers may not offer to drive or walk children/young people anywhere outside the library.**
5. **Volunteers should not initiate discussions of religious, political or sexual matters with any of the children/young people.**
6. **Volunteers should show all non-library material (including "treats") to the Homework Center Coordinator or library staff before using them or presenting them to the children.**
7. **Volunteers should be on time as scheduled, and call the library if they will not be able to work. Volunteers who intend to discontinue participation in the program should promptly notify the Homework Center Coordinator or library staff.**
8. **Volunteers should consult with their individual Homework Center Coordinator or library staff for specific rules regarding that library.**

I have read, and agree to follow, the above guidelines. I understand that refusal to follow any of the above guidelines may be cause for dismissal from my volunteer position.

_____   _____

NAME   **DATE**

BIBLIOTECAS GRÁTIS DEL CONDADO DE MONTEREY
Guía Para Los Voluntarios
Centros de Tarea y Horas de Cuentos

Bienvenido! Nos dá mucho gusto de que se una al personal como voluntario/a en esta sucursal se las Bibliotecas Grátis del Condado de Monterey. Al darse como voluntario/a, usted proveerá soporte educacional a los niños y adolescentes en su comunidad. Al mismo tiempo, será un gran ejemplo para cada niño qu conozca.

Como adultos, al trabajar con los niños y adolescentes en la biblioteca, tenemos la responsabilidad con ellos y con las personas que usan nuestros servicios de ser justos y consistentes con todos y de respetar a todos por igual. Para poder lograr esta experiencia positiva para usted y para los niños, le pedimos que sigan estas sugerencias:

1. Todo contacto entre los voluntarios y los niños/adolescentes debe de ocurrir solamente en la biblioteca.
2. Los voluntarios deben de estar concientes de la dignidad natural y autoestima de cada niño. A cada niño se le enseña por sus padres y maestros que no se dejen tocar por nadie, que no séa algún familiar. Por favor respete esto y no inicie algun contacto personal con ellos.
3. Cualquier problema con un niño debe de reportarse al coordinador/a de Centro de Tarea o al personal de la biblioteca. Ellos resolverán el problema.
4. Los voluntarios no pueden ofrecer a llevár a los niños/adolescentes a ningun lugar fuera de la biblioteca.
5. Los voluntarios no pueden de discutir temas sobre religión, politíca o sexualidad con los niños/adolescentes.
6. Los voluntarios deben de enseñar toda materia que no sea parte de la biblioteca, como regalitos o refrescos al coordinador/a o personal de la biblioteca, antes de dárselo al niño/adolescentes.
7. Los voluntarios deben de llegar a tiempo para la hora designada o avisar si no podrá llegar a trabajar. Los voluntarios que piensan dejar su puesto en el programa deben de notificar al coordinador/a del centro de tarea o al personal de la biblioteca.
8. Los voluntarios deben de consultar con el coordinador/a del centro de tarea o personal de la biblioteca para explicación de reglas especificas en esa biblioteca.

Yo he leído y estoy de acuerdo en seguir las reglas. Yo entiendo de que si me niego a seguir cualquiera de las reglas, puedo ser despedido de mi puesto como voluntario/a.

NOMBRE _____   FECHA _____

VOLUNTEER AGREEMENT

Date: _____

I have attended the Family Technology Learning Center (TLC) Volunteer Training and would like to participate in this program.

I agree to notify the Family TLC Librarian if I must change my schedule, to call a substitute if I must miss my shift and to notify the Family TLC as soon as possible if I must discontinue my service.

_____

Signature

_____

Staff Initials

Math Peer Tutor Agreement

As a math peer tutor, I agree to:

- attend an orientation session at the central library in late September
- arrive at work on time (by 3:55 P.M.) Mondays when public schools are in session from October 1998 through June 1999
- call the Young Adult Services Division (230-2120, 2119) as soon as I know that I will be unable to come to work or will be late
- sign in each Monday when I arrive at the library
- talk to my supervisor if I have any questions or problems

Signed _____

Date _____

The Brooklyn Public Library agrees to:

- introduce you to staff members in Young Adult Services
- register you for a library card, if you need one
- provide an orientation before you begin
- provide a librarian to supervise the program and guide you
- provide a certificate at the end of the year, signed by the director
- have an end of the year party in June!

Signed _____

Date _____

Your school agrees to:

- grant peer tutors high school community service credit for each semester you participate in the program
- note your peer tutoring experience in your high school record

Signed _____

Date _____

94

VOLUNTEER STATEMENT OF COMMITMENT

Name _____

Address (Street) _____

       (City) _____ ZIP _____ Phone _____

As a volunteer in the Multnomah County Library system, I commit myself to:

    Branch/Section _____ for _____ hours

    per   ☐ week   ☐ month for a period of _____ months.

I AGREE:

    To attend orientation and training when necessary.

    To accept guidance and evaluation from the staff advisor and maintain a smooth
       working relationship with all employees.

    To notify the staff advisor by telephone of an absence as far in advance as
       possible.

    To comply with library policies.

IN RETURN THE LIBRARY AGREES:

    To provide a pleasant work environment.

    To provide training when necessary.

    To appreciate the commitment and task accomplished.

Signature _____ Date _____

Date of birth (Month) _____ (Day) _____ (Year) _____

Please return to the Volunteer Coordinator,
Multnomah County Library, 205 N.E. Russell, Portland

MULTNOMAH COUNTY
LIBRARY

95

LEAD HOMEWORK ASSISTANT

JOB DESCRIPTION

The Lead Homework Assistant has the same responsibilities as Homework Assistants for working with students, but in addition the Lead Homework Assistant:

- Supervises registration of students and their parents
- Supervises Homework Assistants, which includes

    assisting them in their work with students
    helping them develop projects
    helping them handle difficult students

- Maintains student records and shares them with library staff and project schools
- May conduct, or assist librarians in conducting, training for Homework Assistants and volunteers
- Assists in planning and presenting group programs for students and/or parents
- Communicates with Library Supervisor/Youth Services Librarian on Center needs, ideas for improvements, etc.
- Orders supplies as needed
- May contact parents and teachers in project schools to:

    publicize Homework Center programs
    request information on school assignments, computer software, etc.
    check on students who don't attend Center as scheduled

Educational Qualifications

Enrolled in Teacher's Education at CSUS (being further along in program than Homework Assistants is desirable); course(s) in Multi-cultural Education

Basic knowledge of computers

Proficiency in reading and math

Proficiency in developing reading and math-related activities

Ability to speak and understand Spanish, Russian or Southeast Asian language is desirable; almost essential

Some direct experience in working with K–8th grade children is desirable

Personal Qualifications

Good organizational and communication skills	Flexibility
	Patience
Creativity	Enjoys working with children

Homework
Alert Center

Homework Alert Center Mentor Job Description

Job Title: Homework Alert Center Mentor

Supervisor: Kim Thompson, School-Library Liaison, 757-6708

Time Commitment: Two shifts per month, each two or three hours long.
More shifts if desired.

Locations: Main Branch, both floors.

Duties and Responsibilities:

> Greet students and make them feel welcome
>
> Help students locate library resources
>
> Check-out of office supplies. Refill if necessary
>
> Straighten centers before leaving

Qualifications and Skills:

> Experience working with children
>
> Desire to help
>
> Ability to communicate
>
> Commitment to the program
>
> Willingness to be trained and to follow library rules and
>   procedures
>
> Patience to explain and teach skills
>
> Enthusiastic, competent and friendly
>
> Belief in value of homework

Requirements: Complete an application and reference check

> Attend two, three-hour training sessions

VOLUNTEER GUIDELINES

Vision
The ASPIRE volunteer program seeks to provide a committed, diverse group of tutors to assist at-risk middle school students with homework and other after school activities. ASPIRE seeks to encourage positive youth development by providing access to caring adults and structured age appropriate programs, materials, and services.

Goals of ASPIRE
1. To provide one-on-one tutoring with volunteers in all subject matters
2. To provide homework assistance and instruction on using library resources
3. To provide access to the Internet, educational software, and other information technology
4. To provide activities such as contests, reading programs, and special events

Job duties:
> Assist students with homework in a wide range of subject areas, including reading, math, and social sciences. Basic reading instruction is often required.
> Help students learn study skills, problem solving, and other techniques to foster their development at students.
> Provide students with positive reinforcement and encouragement, and help them develop an enthusiasm for reading, learning, and library use.
> Assist the ASPIRE facilitator in planning, implementing, and evaluating special programs and activities.
> Assist the ASPIRE facilitator with helping students finding information in the library or by using electronic resources, such as the Internet.
> Assist the ASPIRE facilitator in creating a positive learning environment

Supervision
The branch ASPIRE facilitator will be responsible for the training, supervision, and evaluation of ASPIRE tutors. In the absence of the ASPIRE facilitator, tutors should report to the branch manager and/or the branch volunteer coordinator.

Orientation and training
Each ASPIRE tutor will receive an orientation to ASPIRE, the branch library, and the Houston Public Library. In this orientation and subsequent training, tutors will learn about items such as:
> Tour of the branch/introduction of staff
> Scheduling and recording/reporting work
> Name tags, dress guidelines and other work rules
> Routines, day-to-day activities, and keeping statistics
> Basic library instruction and Internet instruction (if needed)
> Basic Computer and printer problem solving
> Guidelines for Internet use, appropriate behavior, and referral to library staff
> Expectations of volunteers, evaluation, and recognition.

Time commitment
ASPIRE tutors are asked to commit to at least two volunteers hours per week. Tutors are asked to make a commitment to ASPIRE for at least four months.

98

Minneapolis Public Library
Homework Helper Program
Guidelines for Tutor

Primary Purpose:
Homework Helper tutors in ten community libraries throughout Minneapolis provide one-to-one, drop-in tutorial assistance for elementary, middle and high school students. The program is designed to help students with homework assignments, improve their skills, provide computers with word processing capabilities, give access to the library's webcat and a wide range of materials, and provide basic school supplies. Tutors serve as mentors and role models to the students who come in for help.

Responsibilities:
Guide students in completing homework assignments.
- Follow basic tutoring principles
- Set goals with students, if appropriate, and communicate with parent/caregiver about student goals and progress
- Contact teachers, if needed, to provide additional information about assignments

Assist students in library research.
- Apply basic information about resources available at the library for students' use
- Be able to guide students in the library's on-line catalog
- Be able to order materials from other libraries
- Ask a librarian for assistance as appropriate

Facilitate the use of Homework Helper computers.
- Supervise students in use of the computer
- If necessary, impose time limits for computer use
- Implement the library's internet policies
- Contact the SOS Technology Department as needed for technical assistance

Promote the Homework Helper Program.
- Complete monthly reports, including statistical reports, as requested
- While in communication with the community librarian, complete outreach within the library and within the library's community

Serve as a mentor.
- Assist young people in becoming the best they can be
- Listen to and talk with students about current issues, and offer referral to appropriate resources, if asked
- Model respect, tolerance, cooperation, and other positive values

Assist staff in daily library operations.
- Be part of a safe, positive and welcoming atmosphere in the library
- When time permits, assist staff with miscellaneous tasks

There are resources to assist you in all these roles, from tutoring to mentoring to promoting the Homework Helper program. Regular tutor meetings are scheduled for support and training, which tutors are expected and paid to attend. Meetings will be held at various branches. The program manager and the tutor manual are other resources for tutors.

Finally, library staff is also available to talk with and to provide direction. Your direct supervisor and "first contact for help" is the Community or District Librarian. While the tutor is the person primarily responsible for running the Homework Helper program at each branch, your supervisor will work with you regarding any issues or situations of concern that arise while tutoring. If you have any other questions, please contact Sara Waters, Homework Helper Program Coordinator, 612-630-6490.

East Palo Alto Learning Support Program
"Libraries Now, Success Now"

Description:

The County Library will provide a learning support and mentoring program at the East Palo Alto Library that offers a safe location for teens to gather where supportive role models will assist them with their homework needs and help build educational skills. The program will be open to all students, but staff will work intensively with a core group of youth-at-risk.

Statement of Need:

The population for East Palo Alto is 25,050 (1997 estimate based on 1990 census data) and has the highest concentration of youth, ages 13–17 in the County. The ethnic make-up is 41% African-American, 36% Hispanic, 12% White and 9% Pacific Islander. The high school dropout rate in the Sequoia School District is 57.94% Hispanic and 14.65% African-American.

East Palo Alto does not have a public high school. Teens are bused to several high schools, but return home shortly after school where the East Palo Alto Library currently serves as a hangout. The Library does not have the staff resources to provide the intensive homework help that the students need. Many students are lacking basic educational and language skills. Without these basic skills and homework support, students are less likely to succeed in school, which directly relates to their ability to be prepared for society as adults. There is currently no agency in East Palo Alto that offers a learning program with the extensive school support resources that the library can provide.

Objectives:

- Through referrals from teachers, social service workers and East Palo Alto agencies identify and recruit at-risk youth who would benefit by this program.

- Maintain a regular core of twenty at-risk student participants.

- Attract a monthly average of fifty drop-in teen participants through publicity to the general community.

- Operate the program at peak after-school hours, 3–6 P.M., Monday through Friday during the regular school year.

- Recruit volunteers from area businesses, corporations and Stanford University student organizations.

- Determine educational support library collection gaps by obtaining curriculum expectations from schools serving East Palo Alto teens, and then purchase materials (traditional as well as technological resources) to fill those gaps.

- Identify participants needing specific help with reading and/or English to ensure that they receive tutoring designed to meet their individual needs.

- Solicit donations from businesses for needed school supplies, program incentives and to increase community buy-in.

- Set appropriate individual goals with regular participants, then monitor student progress on a quarterly basis.

- Provide a community event to honor student participants who complete the program.

- Create a manual for replicating this program in other communities.

Timeline

July 1998	Hire a bilingual staff member to coordinate the program.
	Evaluate collection and make recommendations for increased educational support subject areas.
August 1998	Establish contact with all public and private high schools that have East Palo Alto students.
	Identify and connect with agencies, churches and other community organizations that work with teens.
	Hire a tutor.
	Recruit and train volunteers.
September 1998	Acquire additional computers for increased information search.
	Open for use by all students.
	Identified gaps in collection will be filled.
October 1998	At least ten regular attending students will be enrolled in the program.
December 1998	Twenty regular attending students will be enrolled in the program.
June 1999	Honor student participants.
	Conduct and compile evaluation measures.
July 1999	Create a manual for program replication.

(continued)

Performance measures

1. Staff will establish relationships with at least 15 schools, agencies and community organizations that work with East Palo Alto teens and acquire 30 potential referrals.

2. 80% of those enrolled in the program will improve their grade point average by .3 points.

3. A monthly average of fifty drop-in students will attend the program and when surveyed, 85% will report that the program was very helpful in completing their school assignments.

4. 75% of the regular participants will answer yes to a survey question asking if they feel more positive about their chances for educational success than before entering the program.

5. 80% of the regular participants surveyed will report that they feel more positive about themselves and their abilities.

Ronald McDonald Children's Charities of the Bay Area
GRANT APPLICATION FORM

Background and Significance

a. organization background

The Friends of the Foster City Library is a public membership organization which supports the Library's overall purpose by providing program, furnishing and resource enhancements not covered in the Library's budget, and by speaking out on behalf of the Library on issues which directly relate to the Library's ability to serve the ever-changing needs of the community.

The San Mateo County Library provides resources and services to meet not only Foster City's informational, educational, cultural and recreational needs, but as it is a County Library, these services extend to all County residents as well. The library contributes to the development of an informed citizenry and to the growth and transformation of the individual and the community.

b. achievements

The Friends of the Foster City Library is currently raising funds to furnish a new Foster City Library and we were a significant influence in the project's coming to fruition. To date we have raised almost $250,000 for this project. We have also previously raised funding, through book sales and programs, for various library needs such as the summer reading program and monthly children's programming.

Target Audience and Performance Sites
2,679 Foster City youth, ages 8–17
Foster City Library in Foster City, California

a. demographics

Foster City, a planned community, is located midway between San Francisco and San Jose on the western shore of San Francisco Bay and east of 101. Foster City has a population of 29,500 with a projected population of 34,000 by the year 2005. The city encompasses 2,619 acres. Ethic diversity is high.

Families outnumber single persons in Foster City. There are four public schools (elementary and middle) with a total enrollment of 2,679 and one private school with an enrollment of 22. The Foster City Library has heavy demand for school related support, from the elementary level and upwards. Approximately thirty percent of the Library's collection is comprised of juvenile materials. Their annual circulation of materials is approximately 103,954 with juvenile materials making up almost thirty-five percent of the total. The new library site and facility will make it the "flagship" of the county's system.

(continued)

Description of Project: After-School Homework Center

a. description of need

Foster City needs an after-school homework center for its children. Currently, Foster City school libraries do not have the staff or funding to provide this on a school site. The principal at Brewer Island Elementary estimates that ninety percent of corrective student conferences are due to a lack of homework support contributing to lowered academic achievement. Additionally, parents of students do not have an avenue to communicate with schools and teachers when there is a lack of understanding of student homework assignments.

b. why our program will make a difference

An after-school homework center will provide youth with a safe environment that is conducive to study and learning. The library will make available the resources to meet student's homework needs. Staff will provide students with after-school homework assistance that will promote academic improvement. Academic success is a proven and primary factor for success in life.

Foster City is building an 18,500 sq. ft. facility to replace the current 4,800 sq. ft. library which reached capacity in 1985. The new library will be an ideal site for this program. It will be centrally located, will service the entire student community and the larger building will have a room available to easily accommodate a program of this nature. Also, based on current use, the primary role of the Foster City Library is educational support making it a good match for the many students who need this type of support. It is based on successful programs at Pacifica and Redwood city libraries and on models throughout the country. Our project has the support of Foster City School administration and Foster City P.T.A. organizations.

c. specific purpose of funds

Funding from your organization will be reserved solely for the Homework Center. San Mateo County Library has experienced considerable budget problems over the last few years with a forty percent drop in funding. Currently, the Foster City Friends fund raising is committed to the new building, so funding the after-school homework center at this time is not possible, but after three years, the Foster City Friends of the Library will assume responsibility for the program. Foster City Schools do not have the budget to provide this service either. Unless outside sources of revenue are found, the new library will not be able to provide this service to the community.

Objectives and Goals

a. *Goal:*

Promote academic excellence to children and youth in Foster City.

Objective:

Offer a safe, easily accessible environment that facilitates learning to youth.

Objective:

Provide trained staff and volunteers to deliver after-school homework assistance that will promote academic improvement.

Objective:

Supply books, technology and other materials necessary to facilitate learning.

b. strategies

The hours of the center will be during established critical student use times from 3 P.M. to 5 P.M., four days a week, Monday through Thursday. The center will be staffed during these times with one certified teacher who will be responsible for soliciting and scheduling additional volunteers and who will be responsible for maintaining communication with teachers regarding school assignments. Materials and equipment will be purchased to support our goals and will be accessible to children during the hours of the center and whenever the library is open.

Evaluation

The teacher hired for this project will be responsible for gathering evaluative data. At the end of the year, this person will assess the degree upon which our project goals and objectives have been realized. In order to facilitate this, the program teacher will design evaluation instruments (such as surveys to use with teachers, parents and students) that will determine the homework center's effectiveness.

Previous Donor Information

Family TLC User Agreement

- Sign in and out at the registration desk.

- Clean hands before using equipment.

- Observe the no food, drinks or chewing gum policy.

- Follow rules concerning behavior.

- Sessions are for one hour.

- No outside discs or software – a 3.5" floppy disc will be provided for each user.

- No unattended young children are to be left in the lab.

- Sign in and out for software and return it when finished.

- E-mail, games and chat rooms are considered unacceptable use of the Family TLC.

- Internet access is unfiltered. Minors must have signed parental approval before going online.

I understand I may lose access to the Family TLC if I break my agreement.

USER _____ DATE _____

STAFF _____

SACRAMENTO PUBLIC LIBRARY AUTHORITY
MARTIN LUTHER KING LIBRARY
HOMEWORK CENTER
7340 24th Street Bypass
Sacramento, CA 95822

STUDENT REGISTRATION

Program information: The Homework Center provides homework assistance to students in grades K through 8. Homework Center hours are: 3 p.m. to 7 p.m. Monday through Thursday. Registered students will be assigned two one-hour sessions a week, and can also "drop in" on other days on a first-come, first-served basis. <u>Students must have a library card to participate.</u>

Student's name_____Grade_____Age_____

Address_____City & Zip_____

Phone: (Home)_____(Work)_____

Name of Parent or Guardian (please print):_____

IN CASE OF EMERGENCY, if parent or guardian cannot be reached, please call:

Name:_____Phone (Home)_____(Work)_____

Language spoken at home:_____ Birthdate:_____

Teacher's name:_____ School Attended_____

I GIVE PERMISSION FOR MY CHILD TO PARTICIPATE IN HOMEWORK CENTER ACTIVITIES

Yes   No

☐   ☐   My child may be photographed for Homework Center publicity.

☐   ☐   My child's school/teacher may be contacted for information on his/her progress (test scores, attitude toward school, attendance data, etc.).

☐   ☐   My child may eat snacks when they are available. He/she is allergic to_____

ADULT COMMITMENT: My child and I know that library rules must be followed or he/she will be asked to go home for the day. I know that the Homework Center is not a child-care program. I will do all that I can to make sure that my child//ward attends regularly at the times agreed upon. My child will bring his/her homework and school materials to the Library.

_____
Signature of parent or guardian

STUDENT COMMITMENT: I will remember to bring my school work with me to the Homework Center. I know that I must follow the library rules and behave calmly, quietly and politely. If I do not behave appropriately, the Library staff will ask me to go home for the day.

TODAY'S DATE_____   _____
Signature of Student

107

AUTORIDAD DE BIBLIOTECAS PÚBLICAS DE SACRAMENTO
BIBLIOTECA MARTIN LUTHER KING
CENTRO PARA TAREAS ESCOLARES
7340 24TH Street Bypass
Sacramento, CA 95822

REGISTRO DE ESTUDIANTES

Información del programa: El Centro para Tareas Escolares ofrece apoyo para las tareas escolares a estudiantes en los grados K a 8. El horario del Centro para Tareas Escolares es de 3 p. m. a 7 p. m., de lunes a jueves. A los estudiantes registrados se les asignarán dos sesiones de una hora por semana y también pueden llegar al Centro otros días, donde se les atenderá según vayan llegando. Para participar, los estudiantes deberán presentar su credencial de la biblioteca.

Nombre del estudiante _____ Grado_____ Edad_____

Idioma que se habla en casa_____ Fecha de nacimiento_____

Nombre del maestro _____ Escuela_____

Nombre del padre, madre o tutor (en letra de molde) _____

Dirección_____ Ciudad/Zona postal_____

Teléfono (casa)_____ (trabajo) _____

EN CASO DE EMERGENCIA, si no se puede localizar al padre o tutor, favor de llamar a:

Nombre_____

Teléfono (casa)_____ (trabajo) _____

DOY MI PERMISO A MI HIJO PARA QUE PARTICIPE EN LAS ACTIVIDADES DEL CENTRO PARA TAREAS ESCOLARES:

Sí   No
☐   ☐   Pueden fotografiar a mi hijo para la publicidad del Centro para Tareas Escolares.

☐   ☐   Pueden ponerse en contacto con el maestro o la escuela para pedir información del desempeño de mi hijo (calificaciones, actitud hacia la escuela, asistencia, etc.).

☐   ☐   Mi hijo puede comer bocadillos cuando se tengan disponibles. Mi hijo es alérgico a:

_____.

COMPROMISO DEL ADULTO: Mi hijo y yo sabemos que se deben seguir las reglas de la biblioteca, o de lo contrario se le pedirá que se vaya a casa el resto del día. Sé que el Centro para Tareas Escolares no es un programa de atención infantil. Haré todo lo que pueda para asegurar que mi hijo asista con regularidad en el horario acordado. Mi hijo llevará su tarea y los materiales de la escuela a la biblioteca.

_____
Firma del padre, madre, o tutor

COMPROMISO DEL ESTUDIANTE: Me acordaré de traer mi trabajo de la escuela al Centro para Tareas Escolares. Sé que debo seguir las reglas de la biblioteca y portarme de manera tranquila, callada y con cortesía. Si no me porto de la manera apropiada, el personal de la biblioteca me pedirá que me vaya a casa el resto del día.

_____   _____
Firma del estudiante   *Fecha de hoy*

M104   COM 7/98

108

ЦЕНТР ПОМОЩИ С ДОМАШНИМ ЗАДАНИЕМ В БИБЛИОТЕКЕ МАРТИНА ЛЮТЕРА КИНГА

7340 24th Street Bypass
Sacramento, CA 95822

РЕГИСТРАЦИЯ УЧЕНИКОВ

Информация о программе: Центр Помощи с Домашним Заданием предоставляет помощь ученикам с дошкольного по 8 класс. Часы работы центра: с 3:00 до 7:00 вечера со вторника по четверг, и с 3:00 до 5:00 дня по пятницам, в дни, когда работает библиотека. Зарегистрированным ученикам будут назначены два занятия в неделю по одному часу, они также могут приходить за помощью в другие дни. Ученики должны иметь библиотечную карточку для участия в программе.

Имя ученика: _____ Класс: _____ Возраст: _____

Адрес: _____ Город и индекс: _____

Телефон: домашний _____ рабочий: _____

Имя родителя/опекуна: _____

В СЛУЧАЕ ЧРЕЗВЫЧАЙНОЙ СИТУАЦИИ, если до родителей или опекунов невозможно дозвониться, звонить:
Имя: _____ Телефон: дом. _____ раб. _____

На каком языке говорят дома: _____ День рождения: _____

Имя учителя: _____ В какую школу ходит: _____

Я ДАЮ РАЗРШЕНИЕ МОЕМУ РЕБЕНКУ УЧАСТВОВАТЬ В РАБОТЕ ЦЕНТРА ПО ПОМОЩИ С ДОМАШНЕЙ РАБОТОЙ:

Да   Нет
☐   ☐   Я разрешаю моему ребенку быть сфотографированным для рекламы центра.
☐   ☐   Я разрешаю звонить учителю моего ребенка, чтобы узнать о его успехах (результаты тестов, отношение к учебе, посещение школы и т.д.)
☐   ☐   Мой ребенок может перекусить в библиотеке, когда там предлагают еду. У него/ее есть аллергия на: _____.

ЗАМЕТКА ДЛЯ ВЗРОСЛЫХ: Мой ребенок и я понимаем, что мы должны соблюдать правила поведения в библиотеке, иначе моего ребенка попросят уйти домой. Я понимаю, что программа помощи с дом. заданием не является программой по развлечению детей. Я сделаю все от меня зависящее, чтобы мой ребенок посещал библиотеку во все назначенные часы. Мой ребенок принесет его/ее домашние задания и школьные материалы в библиотеку.

Подпись родителя/опекуна: _____

ЗАМЕТКА ДЛЯ УЧЕНИКОВ: Я буду всегда приносить мое домашнее задание в Центр Помощи с Домашним заданием. Я понимаю, что я должен соблюдать правила поведения в библиотеке, вести себя тихо и спокойно, вежливо. Если я не буду вести себя спокойно, работники библиотеки попросят меня уйти домой.

Дата: _____ Подпись ученика: _____

Tigard-Tualatin School District
13137 S.W. Pacific Hwy.
Tigard, OR 97223
620-1620

Tigard Public Library
13125 SW Hall Blvd.
Tigard, OR 97223
684-6537

Homework Center Permission Slip
Tigard Public Library

The Tigard Public Library and the Tigard-Tualatin School District cannot be responsible for the whereabouts of your child while attending the Homework Center. We can verify if a student has taken the bus to the Tigard Library, but we cannot prevent a student from leaving the library nor can we ensure that a student goes to the library after taking the bus to the library. We encourage you to make these arrangements and reach an understanding with your child concerning responsible attendance and use of the Homework Center.

If children are left at the Tigard Library after closing at 9:00 p.m., the Tigard Police Department will be contacted: this is for the child's safety.

If students cannot follow the rules of the Homework Center and are asked to leave on a particular day, a Tigard Library staff member will notify the parent or guardian and the child will make appropriate arrangements.

_____

Date: _____Student's Name: _____

School: _____

I, the parent/guardian of the above named student, understand the above conditions, and grant permission to the school to take him/her to the Tigard Public Library's Homework Center during its hours of operation. I also agree to be responsible for making arrangements for my child to be picked up at the Tigard Public Library during operating hours.

Signature of Parent/Guardian: _____

Address: _____

Home Phone: _____   Work Phone: _____

MEDICAL WAIVER
I, the parent/guardian of the above named student, grant permission to the supervising staff to provide necessary medical services in an emergency if I cannot be contacted using the above numbers.

Signature of Parent/Guardian: _____

110

¿Necesita su hijo o hija ayuda con la tarea?
¿Faltan las materiales escolares: papel, lapices y
plumas, cuaderno, cartulina, tijeras etc.?

La Biblioteca Latinoamericana está empezando
El Club de la Tarea
de lunes a jueves
de 4:00 a 6:00 pm

Habrán voluntarios para ayudar con las tareas y utensilios escolares
para hacerlas. También los estudiantes del club podrán sacar
fotocopias de los materiales que se necesiten para sus trabajos escolares.

Por favor, pida información a cualquier empleado de la Biblioteca o llame al 294-1237.

Does your son or daughter need help with homework?
Do you lack school supplies at home such as paper,
pens and pencils, notebooks, scissors, etc.?

The Biblioteca (Latin American Library) is starting a
Homework Club
Monday through Thursday
4:00 - 6:00 pm

There will be volunteers who will help with homework, and there will
be school supplies available. Also, students will be able to make
free photocopies of materials needed for homework.

For more information ask a library employee or call the Biblioteca at 294-1237.

Source: San Jose Public Library, California.

Need help with your homework?

Come to the Library!

The New Rochelle Public Library
offers free homework help
Mondays through Thursdays
3:30 p.m. to 5:00 p.m.
through three programs:

America Reads Challenge
Provided by funding from the Federal Work-Study Program at the College of New Rochelle

Teacher in the Library
Funded by the City School District of New Rochelle

Bi-Lingual Help (English & Spanish)
Provided by a grant from the Community Development Block Grant Program of the U.S.
Department of Housing and Urban Development through the City of New Rochelle

¿Necesita ayuda con su tarea?

Venga a la Biblioteca!

La Biblioteca Pública de New Rochelle
ofrece ayuda gratis
Lunes a Viernes
3:30 p.m. a 5:00 p.m.
patronisado por:

America Reads Challenge
Provided by funding from the Federal Work-Study Program at the College of New Rochelle

Teacher in the Library
Funded by the City School District of New Rochelle

Bi-Lingual Help (English & Spanish)
Provided by a grant from the Community Development Block Grant Program of the U.S. Department of Housing and Urban Development through the City of New Rochelle

Is Your Homework Driving You Crazy?

Get help with your homework at Tigard Library's Homework Center, staffed by tutors who can help you tackle your assignments.

Where: Tigard Public Library

When: Mondays, Tuesdays, and Wednesdays from 4:00 – 6:00 p.m., starting October 4, 1999 through May 2000.

How: Get your parents to sign the permission slip so you can take the bus after school or get a ride from a friend.

Who: Middle school and high school students.

What: Bring your assignments and your brain.

Why: Everyone needs help with homework. Call Marin Younker, 684-6537 x283, if you have questions.

Tigard Public Library
13125 SW Hall Blvd.
Tigard, OR 97223
Phone: (503) 684-6537
Fax: (503) 598-7515

114

FREE MATH Homework HELP

Help for middle school and high school students

Get help on a drop-in, first come, first served basis from volunteer tutors

ALGEBRA GEOMETRY TRIGONOMETRY CALCULUS and BASIC MATH
for secondary students

MONDAY nights, 7-9 PUBLIC LIBRARY
Monroe Co. Public Library, 303 E. Kirkwood, 2nd fl., Rm B.

WEDNESDAY nights, 7-9 McDONALD'S WEST
2910 West 3rd St., Corner of Highway 37and West 3rd St.

This Partnership Project is funded and sponsored by:
Monroe County Public Library, McDonald's Restaurants, Monroe County Education Association,
and the Monroe County Community School Corporation.

Questions, schedule, additional information: Call the library's reference desk: 349-3228

Brooklyn
Public
Library

Dear Math Teacher,

The Central Library Youth Services Division of the Brooklyn Public Library offers a Math Peer Tutoring Program for middle school and high school students every Monday, 4-5 P.M., when the public high schools are in session.

Eleventh and twelfth grade peer tutors who have been recommended by their high school math teachers volunteer one hour each week to provide one on one tutoring for students who need help in mathematics.

We recommend that students bring their math homework, textbook or a math test they wish to review with a tutor. The program is free, and tutors are available on a first come, first served basis. We currently have (number) peer tutors who have been able to accommodate all participants, thus far.

Please post one of the enclosed flyers outside the Math Department Office, and distribute the remaining flyers to math teachers so that they can inform students of this highly successful program.

Thank you for your time and cooperation. Please call me if you have any questions regarding the program. My number is . . .

Sincerely,

Tools for Assessing Effectiveness

PASS!—Partners for Achieving School Success
A Project of the Oakland Public Library

_____Name

_____Branch

SITE COORDINATOR EVALUATION—1996

Hi everyone!

This is the "end of the year assessment" that will assist us in making modifications to the *PASS!* program during the summer so that we have a better, more effective program when we begin again next Fall. Please answer the questions as fully as possible based on your experiences. You may well have information that you wish to share, for which there is not a question included. Feel free to add it at the end. This is your opportunity to tell me all those things you think I should know. Everything is of value. If not all questions apply to you, answer those that do. Thank you.

1. Do you believe that the *PASS!* program (including you, your mentors and your students) was integrated into your library's regular ongoing programs and services? Why? Why not?

2. What suggestions and recommendations would you offer to the branch staff to help integrate the *PASS!* program more fully into the life of the branch?

3. What is the basic age group, grade level served by your homework center?

_____ Grades 1-2   _____ Grades 5-6

_____ Grades 3-4   _____ Grades 7-8

                                         _____ Other (specify)

(continued)

4. What academic skills seem to be those most needed by the students seeking help?

     _____ Reading   _____ Science

     _____ Math   _____ Social studies

     _____ Spelling   _____ Other

5. What additional materials do you think would benefit the program?

6. What teaching aids have you found particularly effective? Include everything you have used <u>besides</u> what the kids have brought in as part of their homework. Include worksheets, newspaper stuff, etc. Feel free to include samples.

7. What suggestions do you have for dealing with children who have finished their homework? How can we avoid becoming a child-care center? Is this a concern?

8. Is participation in *PASS!* making a difference for the students attending the program? How?

9. What have been <u>your</u> greatest challenges during this project?

10. What additional training do you think you need to be a more effective site coordinator?

11. What additional training do your high school mentors need in order to work effectively with the younger students?

12. What sorts of activities do you and your mentors do with students to make their work meaningful to them?

13. What suggestions do you have for interview questions for the mentors when we hire them in the summer?

14. What interview questions should we add to those we ask of prospective site coordinators that would reflect the skills actually needed on this job? Yes, I have used questions from this answer.

15. The program has required some documentation. Do you have any suggestions for modification or revision? Suggest any changes that you wish.

16. How can we get more parent input and participation?

17. Is there anything else you want to add?

Thank you very much for taking the time to fully answer everything. I appreciate your thoughts, observations and concerns, as well as all the flexibility that you have brought to this project at your site. *It has been wonderful working this you this year!*

PASS!—Partners for Achieving School Success
A Project of the Oakland Public Library

_____Name

_____Branch

HOMEWORK MENTOR QUESTIONNAIRE—1996

Hi everyone!

This is the "end of year assessment" that will assist us in making modifications to the *PASS!* program during the summer so that we have a better, more effective program when we begin again next Fall. Please answer the questions as fully as possible based on your experiences. You may well have information that you wish to share, for which there is not a question included. Feel free to add it at the end. This is your opportunity to tell me all those things you think I should know. Everything is of value. If not all questions apply to you, answer those that do. Thank you.

1. Are you interested in working with the *PASS!* program next year? Why? Why not? I do realize that your plans may change over the summer.

2. If yes to the above question, do you wish to remain at your current site or would you like to work with a different site? Which site, if all else equal? Why?

3. What have been <u>your</u> greatest challenges during this project?

4. How have you benefited from working for *PASS!*?

5. What suggestions and recommendations would you offer to the branch staff to help the *PASS!* program be more a part of the branch?

120

6. What is the basic age group, grade level served by your homework center?

   _____ Grades 1-2   _____ Grades 5-6
   _____ Grades 3-4   _____ Grades 7-8
                                              _____ Other (specify)

7. What academic skills seem to be those most needed by the students seeking help?

   _____ Reading   _____ Science
   _____ Math   _____ Social studies
   _____ Spelling   _____ Other

8. What suggestions do you have for dealing with children who have finished their homework?

9. What teaching aids have you found particularly effective? Include everything you have used <u>besides</u> what the kids have brought in as part of their homework. Include worksheets, newspaper stuff, etc. Feel free to include samples.

10. What additional study materials do you think would benefit the program?

11. Is participation in *PASS!* making a difference for the students attending the program? How?

12. Have the training sessions provided by Youth Employment and/or *PASS!* on Friday afternoons been helpful? What topics would you like included for next year?

13. What suggestions do you have for interview questions for the students we will hire for next year?

14. What else would you like to add?

Thank you very much for taking the time to fully answer everything. I appreciate your thoughts, observations and concerns, as well as all the flexibility that you have brought to this start-up project at your site. *You have been a pleasure to work with this year!*

PASS!—Partners for Achieving School Success
A Project of the Oakland Public Library

TEACHER QUESTIONNAIRE

As part of its services to children, the Oakland Public Library operates homework programs in nine branch libraries. During the past school year at least one of your students have been participating in the *PASS!* after school homework program. At the end of each academic year we try to collect information about our effectiveness. Please take a few moments to fill out the questionnaire below and return it to me in the enclosed stamped envelope. If you have any questions at all, feel free to telephone me at XXXXXXX. In advance, many thanks for your assistance and support!

—Barbara S. Alesandrini, *PASS!* Project Coordinator

- Did you know that homework assistance is provided in 9 branch libraries?   Yes   No   Unsure

- Did you know that your student participated in the *PASS!* after school homework assistance program?   Yes   No   Unsure

- While attending *PASS!*, did your student complete his/her homework on a regular basis?   Yes   No   Unsure

- Did you notice an improvement in the completion rate of your student's homework?   Yes   No   Unsure

- Did you notice an improvement in your student's confidence or attitude?   Yes   No   Unsure

- Did your student's grades improve by attending the *PASS!* program?   Yes   No   Unsure

- How often do you assign homework?   Daily   2-3 times per week   Once a week

- Does your school provide an after school homework program?   Yes   No   Unsure

- If so, how often?   Daily   2-3 times per week   Once a week

- Do you know of other homework assistance programs in your area?   Yes   No   Unsure

- If yes, please share as much information as you have. We are trying to develop a list of Oakland after school homework programs. Please use other side.

- What suggestions do you have for improving the *PASS!* program?

Name (optional)   School _____ Grade _____

PASS!—Partners for Achieving School Success
A Project of the Oakland Public Library

_____Name

_____Branch

VOLUNTEER PROGRAM EVALUATION—1996

- What time commitment did you make to *PASS!?*

  _____ 1–2½ hours per week

  _____ 2½–4 hours per week

  _____ 4–6 hours per week

- For the following questions, please circle the answer that most appropriately reflects your experience:

	Yes, definitely				No, not at all
• This was a good volunteer assignment for me.	1	2	3	4	5
• I would like to return in the Fall.	1	2	3	4	5
• I made a difference for at least one child with whom I worked.	1	2	3	4	5
• Working conditions were comfortable.	1	2	3	4	5
• I received adequate training.	1	2	3	4	5
• I received appropriate supervision.	1	2	3	4	5

- I would like to be assigned to the following branch if there is a need there. Please indicate your first and second choices.

  _____ Brookfield   _____ Latin American   _____ Melrose

  _____ Elmhurst   _____ Main Lib.—Children's   _____ Temescal

  _____ Golden Gate   _____ Martin Luther King, Jr.   _____ West Oakland

What suggestions do you have for improving the *PASS!* program? Please use the back for more space.

Thank you for taking the time to fully answer everything. We value your contributions and input while we continue developing the best program possible.

TUTOR EVALUATION

Date: _____ Tutor: _____

Session Time In: _____ Time Out: _____

Age of child: _____ Grade: _____ School: _____

Had the child ever used the homework Center before?   YES   NO

How were you approached to help this child? (by child, by parents, by librarian)

What was the child's question? (problem with assignment, using a resource, reading . . .)

How did you assist the child?

Did you feel you were successful? What worked well? What would you do differently next time?

Did you refer the child to anyone else for further assistance? If so, who?

SOURCE: Monroe County Public Library, Indiana.

124

MATH PEER TUTOR EVALUATION

1. As a math peer tutor, I was able to use my skills to help other students understand math concepts and problems.

   _____every week   _____most weeks   _____once in a while   _____never

2. The act of explaining concepts, and providing examples for math problems, helped to strengthen my own math skills.

   _____agree   _____not sure   _____disagree

3. Working as a peer tutor was all that I expected it to be.

   _____agree   _____not sure   _____disagree

4. I enjoyed the experience of being a math peer tutor.

   _____agree   _____not sure   _____disagree

5. I am interested in being a math tutor next year.

   _____yes   _____no

6. I would recommend the math peer tutor experience to a friend.

   _____yes   _____no   _____Why not?

7. I would recommend that a friend or acquaintance who needed help with mathematics come to the math peer tutoring center for help.

   _____yes   _____no   _____Why not?

Next year we hope this program will be even bigger and better. Please take a few minutes to brainstorm ideas for how to improve the math peer tutoring center in the future. Please use the back of this sheet, if necessary.

_____

SOURCE: Brooklyn Public Library, Central Library Youth Services Division.

Homework

Alert Center

Mentor Log

Date: _____   Time: _____   Volunteer Name: _____

****

Student's grade and school:

- Was the student satisfied with library resources?

- What did the student need that we didn't have?

- What did you need that you didn't have?

****

Student's grade and school:

- Was the student satisfied with library resources?

- What did the student need that we didn't have?

- What did you need that you didn't have?

****

Student's grade and school:

- Was the student satisfied with library resources?

- What did the student need that we didn't have?

- What did you need that you didn't have?

****

Student's grade and school:

- Was the student satisfied with library resources?

- What did the student need that we didn't have?

- What did you need that you didn't have?

Naygrow Family Foundation
HOMEWORK CENTER

COLONIAL HEIGHTS COMMUNITY LIBRARY
4799 Stockton Boulevard, Sacramento, CA 95820
A project of the Sacramento Public Library Foundation

PARENT'S EVALUATION

Dear parents, please fill this brief form to help us evaluate our program.

The homework center helps your child in the following ways.   Circle one

Getting their homework done?   Yes/No

Improving their skills?

      In Math   Yes/No
      In Reading   Yes/No
      In Computers   Yes/No
      Other, please list_____

Does your child seem motivated to come to the homework center? Yes/No

Do you feel that the amount of time your child comes to the center is appropriate for his/her
needs?   Yes/No

Does your child find his/her tutor well-trained and helpful?   Yes/No

Please take the time to write any suggestions you might have, or to elaborate on any of the above
questions, so we can help your child better.

_____
_____
_____
_____

Thank you
Maria Elena Griego
Lead Homework Assistant, and Teacher

127

Math Peer Tutoring Center Survey

Place a ✓ in the correct box

1. Current grade:
☐ 7th　　　☐ 8th　　　☐ 9th　　　☐ 10th　　　☐ 11th　　　☐ 12th
☐ other_____

2. Sex:
☐ Male　　　☐ Female

3. ✓ number of times you've been to the Math Peer Tutoring Center:
☐ one　　　☐ two or three　　　☐ four or more

4. ✓ all that apply
I came to math tutoring:
☐ to do my homework　　　☐ because my mother made me　　　☐ to prepare for a test
☐ to go over a test I failed or messed up　　　☐ because my friend was going
☐ because I had nothing else to do　　　☐ other _____

5. ✓ all that apply
I heard about the Math Peer Tutoring Center from:
☐ a friend　　　☐ a parent or guardian　　　☐ a teacher　　☐ a librarian　☐ a flyer
☐ the library calendar of events　　　☐ loudspeaker announcement
☐ other_____

6. Did the tutor help you understand math better than before?
☐ yes　☐ no

7. Did your math grades improve after coming to the Math Peer Tutoring Center?
☐ yes　☐ no　☐ don't know yet

8. Would you recommend it to a friend?
☐ yes　☐ no

9. How many times/week should the library offer after school tutoring?
☐ one ☐ two ☐ three ☐ every day

10. ✓ all that apply
The library should offer after school tutoring in:
☐ biology　　☐ chemistry　☐ Spanish　　☐ French　　☐ writing
☐ other_____

128

Focus-Group Questions

FOCUS GROUP PROTOCOL

PASS! Participants

Reminder: The conversation that these questions hope to stimulate is intended to help us better understand how kids who go to *PASS!* experience the program and improve in school. Please express yourselves honestly. Everything you say will be reported anonymously and compiled with the responses of others.

There are many different reasons why kids go to *PASS!* Each of you has gone at least a few times and some of you are regulars. Let's start by hearing a bit about why you've chosen to go to *PASS!*

1. Why do you go to *PASS!?* (round robin)

    PROBES

    - Safety, indoor activities, parents want them to attend, free, it's close to home, to be around other kids, to use library services (books, computers)
    - Do you know about other after-school programs? Why go to *PASS!* instead of or in addition to these other programs?

Since *PASS!* is held at your neighborhood library, I know you're around books, magazines, and computers.

2. Has being at the library for *PASS!* made you want to read more or use the computer more?

    PROBES

    - Do you ever use the library for fun? (examples)
    - Do you ever use the library for independent (non-homework) reading?
    - Do you know how to find what you want or to get help?
    - Do you ever attend special events (e.g., summer reading games, poetry workshops, book buddies)

Now I want you to think about how things are going for you at school . . . your grades, getting your homework done, finishing projects, attendance . . . things like that.

3. Has *PASS!* helped you at school in any ways?

    PROBE

    - Improved grades, completion of homework, attendance
    - Improved self confidence (e.g., can do homework by oneself or get help)
    - Comments from teachers or parents about perceived improvements

4. What do you like most about *PASS!*
5. What can the library do to make *PASS!* a better program for you?
6. Is there anything that I forgot to ask you about *PASS!* that I should know about?

SOURCE: WestEd, Oakland. *The Oakland Public Library as a Partner in Youth Development: An Evaluation of PASS! and a Needs-Wants Assessment of Library-Linked Youth Development Programs.* Staff report. June 1999.

FOCUS GROUP PROTOCOL
PASS! Mentors

Reminder: The conversation that these questions hope to stimulate is intended to help us better understand *PASS!* and your experiences as a mentor. Please express yourselves honestly. Everything you say will be reported anonymously and compiled with the responses of others.

Let's start by hearing a bit about the program itself.

1. Describe *PASS!* What do you do with the kids? (round robin)

   PROBES

   - Typical activities
   - Biggest challenges
   - Use of technology

2. Do you think *PASS!* helps kids do better at school?

   PROBES

   - Improved academic performance (e.g., grades, homework, attendance)
   - Improved attitude toward school and doing school work
   - Improved social skills (e.g., being resourceful, managing play/study time)
   - New or different types of friendships
   - Do you ever get feedback from their teachers?

3. Do you think *PASS!* inspires kids to use the library?

   PROBES

   - What do they do after they finish their homework?
   - Ever see pleasure reading? Use of the computers?
   - Have you seen them asking questions of the librarians?

4. What's in it for you? What do you get from being a *PASS!* mentor?

   PROBES

   - Money
   - Doing meaningful work
   - Career development skills (see next question)
   - Academic enhancement

5. Can being a *PASS!* mentor help you grow professionally?

   PROBES

   - What general work skills are you learning?
   - What about specific skills (e.g., time management, communication, conflict management, problem solving, contributing at meetings)?
   - What kinds of training or support do you get from Youth Employment Partnership (YEP)?

(continued)

130

6. How are your ideas as mentors included in running the program?

    PROBES

    - Planning the program
    - Having opportunities to be heard and contribute to decisions

7. What are the strengths of the *PASS!* program? What sorts of things do you tell kids or their parents about why they should go to the program?

8. What can the libraries do to make the program better for you and the kids?

9. Is there anything that I forgot to ask you about *PASS!* that I should know about?

SOURCE: WestEd, Oakland. *The Oakland Public Library as a Partner in Youth Development: An Evaluation of* Pass! *and a Needs-Wants Assessment of Library-Linked Youth Development Programs.* Staff report. June 1999.

FOCUS GROUP PROTOCOL
PASS! Parents

Reminder: The conversation that these questions hope to stimulate is intended to help us better understand how you view your kid's experiences with *PASS!* Please express yourselves honestly. Everything you say will be reported anonymously and compiled with the responses of others.

There are many different reasons why kids go to *PASS!* Some of your kids have gone only a few times and others of you have kids that are regulars. Let's start by hearing a bit about why you want your kids to go to *PASS!*

1. Why do you want your kids to go to *PASS!*? (round robin)

    PROBES

    - Safety, indoor activities, parents want them to attend, free, it's close to home, to be around other kids, to use library services (books, computers)
    - Do you know about other after-school programs? Why go to *PASS!* instead of or in addition to these other programs?

Now I want you to think about how things are going for your kids at school . . . their grades, getting homework done, finishing projects, attendance . . . things like that.

2. What have your kids told you about their experiences with *PASS!*?

3. What have you noticed about their school performance since they've been going to *PASS!*?

    PROBES

    - Improved academic performance (e.g., grades, homework, attendance)
    - Improved attitude toward school and doing school work
    - Improved social skills (e.g., being resourceful, managing play/study time)
    - New or different types of friendships

4. What have you noticed about your kid's interest in using the library since they've been involved in *PASS!*?

    PROBES

    - Do they ever use the library for fun? (examples)
    - Do they ever use the library for independent (non-homework) reading?
    - Do they know how to find what they want or to get help?
    - Do they ever attend special events (e.g., summer reading games, poetry workshops, book buddies)?
    - What about you? Have you discovered anything about library services that interests you?

SOURCE: WestEd, Oakland. *The Oakland Public Library as a Partner in Youth Development: An Evaluation of PASS! and a Needs-Wants Assessment of Library-Linked Youth Development Programs.* Staff report. June 1999.

BIBLIOGRAPHY

Adamec, Janet. "Homework Helpers: Making Study Time Quality Time." *Wilson Library Bulletin* 65 (September 1990): 31–32.

American Library Association. *Student Use of Libraries: An Inquiry into the Needs of Students, Libraries, and the Educational Process; Papers of the Conference within a Conference, July 16–18, 1963, Chicago, Illinois.* Chicago: ALA, 1964.

American Library Association. Office for Research and Statistics. *Programs for School-Age Youth in Public Libraries: Report of a Survey Conducted for the DeWitt Wallace–Reader's Digest Fund.* Chicago: ALA, 1999.

Auerbach, Barbara. "Jenny and Her Trig Problem." *School Library Journal* 44 (January 1998): 50.

Bailey, John P. "Quantifying Library Quality: A Homework Center Report Card." *American Libraries* 30 (September 1999): 59–62.

Baird, Jean, and Joan Plessner. "Homework Assistance Centers." *California Libraries* 3 (October 1993): 13.

Brewer, Rosellen. "Help Youth at Risk: A Case for Starting a Public Library Homework Center." *Public Libraries* 31 (July/August 1992): 208–12.

Carnegie Council on Adolescent Development. *Great Transitions: Preparing Adolescents for a New Century.* New York: Carnegie Corporation, 1995.

Carnegie Council on Adolescent Development. *A Matter of Time: Risk and Opportunity in the Nonschool Hours.* New York: Carnegie Corporation, 1992.

Cerny, Roseanne. "An After School Solution." *School Library Journal* 40 (November 1994): 42.

Chelton, Mary K. "Three in Five Public Library Users Are Youth: Implications of Survey Results from the National Center for Education Statistics." *Public Libraries* 36 (March/April 1997): 104–8.

Chelton, Mary K., ed. *Excellence in Library Services to Young Adults.* Chicago: ALA, 1994.

Chelton, Mary K., ed. *Excellence in Library Services to Young Adults.* 2d ed. Chicago: ALA, 1997.

Chelton, Mary K., ed. *Excellence in Library Services to Young Adults: The Nation's Top Programs.* 3d ed. Chicago: ALA, 2000.

Davis, Viki. "Homework Center—Textbooks in the Library." *School Library Journal* 33 (April 1987): 52.

Denny, Carolyn. "Redefining Librarianship: The Case of the Eastside Cybrary Connection." *Public Libraries* 39 (July/August 2000): 208–13.

Dowd, Frances Smardo. *Latchkey Children in the Library and Community: Issues, Strategies, and Programs.* Phoenix, Ariz.: Oryx, 1991.

Dowd, Frances Smardo. "Serving Latchkey Children." *Connect for Kids: Out-of-School Time*. Available at URL: <http://www.connectforkids.org/content1553/content_show.htm?doc_id=8147&attrib_id=318>.

Dunmore, Angela J., and Karen Cropsey Hardiman. "'My Turn' Boosts Teen Self-Esteem: Public Library/Public School Project Ties Students as Tutors." *American Libraries* 18 (October 1987): 786, 788.

Eastman, Linda Anne. "The Children's Room and the Children's Librarian." In *Library Work with Children*, 162–63. Edited by Alice I. Hazeltine. White Plains, N.Y.: H. W. Wilson, 1917. Originally published in *Public Libraries* (1898): 417.

Edwards, Margaret A. *A Fair Garden and the Swarm of Beasts: The Library and the Young Adult*. 1969. Reprint, Chicago: ALA, 1994.

Himmel, Ethel, and William James Wilson. *Planning for Results: A Public Library Transformation Process*. Chicago: ALA, 1998.

"Homework Centers." *Public Library Facts* 2 (March 1999). Available at URL: <http://mlin.lib.ma.us/mblc/sadac/pub_lib_facts_v2-3.shtml>.

"The Institute of Museum and Library Services Responds to Challenge to Help Children Learn." *American Library Association Washington Office Newsline* 8 (August 25, 1999). ALAWON archives available at URL: <http://www.ala.org/washoff/alawon>.

Joint Committee of the National Education Association and the American Library Association. *Schools and Public Libraries: Working Together in School Library Service*. Washington, D.C.: National Education Association of the United States, 1941.

Kassin, Michael. "Tall Tree: Counting the Leaves." *Public Libraries* 38 (March/April 1999): 120–23.

Long, Harriet G. *Rich the Treasure: Public Library Service to Children*. Chicago: ALA, 1953.

Martin, Lowell A. *Students and the Pratt Library: Challenges and Opportunity*. Baltimore: Enoch Pratt Free Library, 1963.

Mediavilla, Cindy. "Homework Assistance Programs in Public Libraries: Helping Johnny Read." In *Young Adults and Public Libraries: A Handbook of Materials and Services*, 181–89. Edited by Mary Anne Nichols and C. Allen Nichols. Westport, Conn.: Greenwood, 1998.

Messineo, Nancy. "'ASSC' and You Shall Receive: Community Partnerships in California." *School Library Journal* 37 (July 1991): 19–22.

Mondowney, JoAnn G. "Licensed to Learn: Drivers' Training for the Internet." *School Library Journal* 42 (January 1996): 32–34.

Moore, Everett. "Serving Students in Time of Crisis." *California Librarian* 2 (October 1961): 219–23.

Morton-Young, Tommie. *After-School and Parent Education Programs for At-Risk Youth and Their Families*. Springfield, Ill.: Charles C. Thomas, 1995.

Newton, Lesley. "The Changing School Curriculum and the Library." *Wilson Bulletin for Librarians* 7 (November 1932): 159.

O'Driscoll, Janis, et al. *A Place of Our Own*. Santa Cruz, Calif.: Santa Cruz City–County Public Libraries, 1997.

Power, Effie L. *Work with Children in Public Libraries*. Chicago: ALA, 1943.

Public Libraries as Partners in Youth Development. New York: DeWitt Wallace–Reader's Digest Fund, [1999].

Rockfield, Gary. "Beyond Library Power: Reader's Digest Adds Public Libraries to the Mix." *School Library Journal* 44 (January 1998): 30–33.

Sager, Don. "Beating the Homework Blues." *Public Libraries* 36 (January/February 1997): 19–23.

Sager, Don. "The Best of Intentions: The Role of the Public Library in the Improvement of Public

Education." *Public Libraries* 31 (January/February 1992): 11–17.

Smith, Duncan, Lynda Fowler, and Alan Teasley. "Homework Help: Problem-Solving through Communication." *North Carolina Libraries* 46 (spring 1988): 33–37.

Sternin, Erica B. "Kids Rule! Libraries Online! Meets High Point Library." *Public Libraries* 37 (July/August 1998): 246–49.

"Teens Talk to America." *The Shell Poll* 1 (summer 1999). Available at URL: <http://www.countoshell.com/shell_poll.html>.

Trotta, Marcia. *Managing Library Outreach Programs: A How-to-Do-It Manual for Librarians.* New York: Neal-Schuman, 1993.

U.S. Department of Commerce. National Telecommunications and Information Administration. *Falling through the Net: Defining the Digital Divide* (November 1999). Available at URL: <http://www.ntia.doc.gov/ntiahome/fttn99/contents.html>.

U.S. Department of Education and U.S. Department of Justice. *Working for Children: Safe and Smart After-School Programs* (April 2000). Available at URL: <http://www.ed.gov/pubs/ parents/ SafeSmart>.

"Urban Libraries Reach Out to Youth." *Connect for Kids: Guidance for Grown-Ups.* Available at URL: <http://www.connectforkids.org/content1553/content_show.htm?doc_id=8006&attrib_id=318>.

Vaillancourt, Renée J. *Bare Bones Young Adult Services: Tips for Public Library Generalists.* Chicago: ALA, 2000.

Walter, Virginia A. *Output Measures and More: Planning and Evaluating Public Library Services for Young Adults.* Chicago: ALA, 1995.

Weisner, Stan. *Information Is Empowering: Developing Public Library Services for Youth at Risk.* Oakland, Calif.: Bay Area Library and Information System, 1992.

WestEd. *The Oakland Public Library as a Partner in Youth Development: An Evaluation of PASS! and a Needs-Wants Assessment of Library-Linked Youth Development Programs.* Oakland: 1999.

Willett, Holly G. *Public Library Youth Services: A Public Policy Approach.* Norwood, N.J.: Ablex, 1995.

INDEX

Cindy Mediavilla currently works for the UCLA Department of Information Studies, where she teaches part-time and oversees special projects. She is also a well-known workshop presenter on topics related to leadership, collection development, and young adult services. For eighteen years, Cindy worked as a public librarian in various libraries throughout Southern California, including the Orange Public Library, where she managed a homework center. In 1998, she received the American Library Association's Loleta D. Fyan Award to study after-school homework-assistance programs across the country. Cindy's doctorate and master's degree in library science are both from UCLA.